RAV DOVBER PINSON

SECRETS OF THE
MIKVAH
סוד המקוה

〜

waters of transformation

Published by IYYUN Publishing
232 Bergen Street
Brooklyn, NY 11217

http:/www.iyyun.com

Iyyun Publishing books may be purchased for educational, business or sales promotional use. For information please contact: contact@IYYUN.com

Editor: Reb Matisyahu Brown

Content Editing: Eden Pearlstein

Proofreading: Alyssa Elbogen

Cover and book design: RP Design and Development

pb ISBN 978-1-7338130-1-3

Pinson, DovBer 1971-
Secrets of the Mikvah: Waters of Transformation
1.Judaism 2. Spirituality 3. Philosophy

SECRETS OF THE
MIKVAH

סוד המקוה

~~~

waters of transformation

RAV DOVBER PINSON

IYYUN PUBLISHING

CONTENTS

OPENING

THERE IS SOMETHING MAGICAL ABOUT WATER. As an element, it both cleanses and quenches, floods and drowns. As a symbol, it implies a state of dream-like fluidity, as well as a sense of hidden depths. When scientists search for life on other planets, they first look for water — without water there is simply no possibility for life as we know it.

It is no coincidence that both the earth's surface, and the structure of the human body, are comprised of around 70 percent water. This symmetry between the planet and the body explains why we are so drawn to oceans, rivers, lakes and springs. Natural bodies of water stir and stimulate the inner worlds and imaginations of children, sailors, mystics and poets alike. They are magnetic and mysterious, simultaneously beckoning and frightening, relaxing and even upsetting for some. Water is our primordial origin. It quietly calls us and all Creation back to the fountains of life deep beneath the surface of consciousness.

For the first 40 days of life, an embryo is called *Mayim b'Alma* / simply water (*Yevamos*, 69b). As a fetus in the womb, our life force is submerged and swims within a sea of warm amniotic waters. Only later, when the waters break, are we birthed onto 'dry land'. This is similar to the Torah's account of Creation. In the beginning, water covers all. Only later do the waters separate, allowing the earth to emerge as a distinct entity, like a tender child.

As water is within us, we yearn to be within it. Entering water can feel like coming home, sinking down into our subconscious mind, or perhaps even unifying with our inner essence.

Whether in constant motion or perfect stillness, each body of water elicits a unique response. Some waters awaken, while others soothe. Similarly, some people are overwhelmingly drawn to water, while others are inexplicably repulsed. The great 16th century Kabbalist known as the Arizal speaks of those whose root soul is connected to Hevel / Abel, that their being close to or immersed in water causes them to feel a heightened sense of love and aliveness. Those whose root soul is connected to Kayin / Cain, by contrast, are irrationally frightened by water, especially by the deeper and darker depths (*Sha'ar haGilgulim*, Hakdamah 36).

In either case, water is undeniably powerful and should therefore be connected to consciously. Towards this end the Torah contains a multitude of *Mitzvos* / Divine precepts and practices that put us into sacred contact with water. Primary among them is the practice of immersing in a Mikvah.

Essentially, a Mikvah is collection of rainwater, wellwater, or certain other bodies of naturally collected water, with certain measurements and qualifications. While this seems quite simple, there are actually vast depths of meaning and power encoded within the details of a Mikvah's form and construction, as well as within the experience of immersion itself.

One of the most basic and powerful aspects of the Mikvah is its power to transform and realign one's state of being. Accordingly, the Torah instructs us to go to the Mikvah when we are out of sync with ourselves, out of balance with our bodies, closed off from other people, shut down to the world, or just vibrating in an erratic pattern. All of these are symptoms or causes of *Tumah* / impurity, as will be explored. This experience of energetic imbalance is an invitation to immerse our misaligned body-mind, which is 70 percent water, into another larger body of water as a means to re-center, re-calibrate, and re-create a healthy equilibrium. Simply put, the Mikvah is Torah's primary means to aid us in reclaiming our original state of spiritual and physical purity.

As we will learn throughout this text, Mikvah is essential for Jewish life, and its power pervades our journey on earth. A person is conceived and begins life after their mother immerses in a Mikvah. Similarly, at the end of their life a person returns to the Mikvah, with the *Teharah* / purification of the body before burial. In between, there are a multitude of needs and uses for the transformative waters of a Mikvah, as will be explored.

The intention of this book is to illuminate the deeper dimensions of the Mitzvah of Mikvah. As with every Mitzvah, there is an *Ohr* / light and a *Kli* / vessel aspect of Mikvah. The Ohr is the soul and *Sod* / inner mystery of the Mikvah. The Kli is its physical dimensions, technicalities, *Halachos* / ritual laws; its *Peshat* / literal dimension. Once we have a firm footing in the exterior details of what constitutes a Mikvah, we can effectively plumb its inner depths. Grasping the Peshat allows us to understand the Sod. This is because Ohr and Kli are really two sides of one reality — both emanating from the *Torah Achas* / the Torah of Oneness, given to us by *Hashem Echad* / the One Divinity, the One Reality. Therefore, we will approach the Mikvah from the outside-in. Before delving into the subtle secrets and spiritual teachings of this exalted Mitzvah, let us begin with the most basic question: What is a Mikvah?

CHAPTER 1

What is a Mikvah?

What is a Mikvah?

A WISE PERSON ONCE SAID THAT THE BEGIN-NING OF WISDOM IS THE DEFINITION OF TERMS. Let us then begin by defining the word *Mikvah*. In the Torah, we first encounter the root of the word *Mikvah* in the beginning of the Creation narrative. Initially, water covered all, from the Heavens to the earth, leaving not a single speck of dust or patch of dry land to stand upon. G-d then said, "Let the water that is beneath the Heavens יקוו / gather into one place [revealing the dry land underneath]. And G-d called the dry land *earth*, ולמקוה / and the *Mikveh* / gathering of the waters, He called *seas*" (*Bereishis*, 1:9-10).

The word *Mikvah* thus means 'gathering', and specifically to a place where water gathers, as another verse says, ומקוה / '...And a Mikvah' you made between the two walls and the water of the old pool" (*Yeshayahu*, 22:11). In a related manner, while discussing various laws pertaining to the defining qualifications of a Mikvah, our Sages use the term *Mayim Ash-Boren* / water gathered in a *Bor* / pit or something similar to a pit (*Taz*, Yoreh De'ah, 201:2). Thus, for a man-made body of water to qualify as a Mikvah fit for ritual immersion, the water must be 'gathered' or stationary and not *Zochalin* / running or moving. Elements such as an operating filter, which continuously circulates the water, render the waters *Zochalin*, and make the Mikvah unfit for use.

Only with natural bodies of springwater can the waters be either flowing or stationary and still qualify as a certified mikvah, for both are natural states of springwater (*Aruch haShulchan*, Yoreh De'ah 201:7).*

However, not just any 'pit' or pool can be used as a Mikvah, according to the Torah it must contain a minimum amount of water which the Sages determined to be a minimum of forty *Sa'ah*. One Sa'ah is about 5 gallons, and 40 Sa'ah is therefore around 198 gallons. The simple reason for this amount is that it takes a minimum of about 40 Sa'ah of water to fully immerse the average human body.

We read in the Torah: "A man from whom there is a discharge of semen shall immerse *all his flesh* in water" (*Vayikra*, 15:16). Our Sages comment, "*All his flesh* in the waters of a Mikvah: this means, in a body of water which *Olah* / covers an entire body. What is its quantity? One *Amah* / cubit square by three cubits high, and the Sages have calculated that the required quantity for a Mikvah is 40 Sa'ah" (*Yuma*, 31a. *Eiruvin*, 4b. *Pesachim*, 109a. This measurement is Torah law, not Rabbinic. *Teshuvas haRivash*, 294. *Aruch haShulchan*, Yoreh De'ah,

---

* There is an opinion that maintains that a *Zavah* / person with certain bodily discharges, needs to immerse in springwater specifically. Rashi brings this opinion, but ultimately rejects it (Rashi, *Shabbos*, 65b. Rashi, *Nidah*, 67a. Although, also see Rashi, *Sanhedrin*, 87a. Rashi, *Bechoros*, 55b. *Zohar* 3, 97b. *Tikkunei Zohar*, Tikkun 5, 143b. *Radak*, Zecharyah, 13:1. *Sefer haEshkol*, Mikvaos, Siman 50). This is not the opinion of all (or most) of the Poskim, as the *Beis Yoseph* writes in *Yoreh De'ah*, 201.

201:6). Interestingly, the word used by *Chazal* / Sages to describe the waters of a Mikvah is *Olah*, which literally means 'elevated'; similarly, a Mikvah that is rendered non-Kosher is called *Yored* / degraded or lowered (for example, *Makos*, 3b). Notably, in various circumstances, the term 'elevated' is also used to imply that one thing is nullified within the presence or substance of another (for example, Mishnah, *Terumos*, 4:7. Rambam, *Hilchos Ma'achalos Asuros*, 16:7). Similarly, as a person submerges within the 40 Sa'ah of water, they cease from breathing for a brief moment and are thereby nullified. This nullification, as we will explore further, is what allows them to be elevated to a new status. Upon emerging from the Mikvah the person then 'stands up' and assumes a new state of being (*Mikvah* has the same letters as *Kumah* / to stand up. *Tikunei Zohar*, p. 37b. *Baal Shem Tov*, Torah, Yisro 11), as will be explored in greater detail.

Today, most people who live in cities do not immerse in springs or wells, but rather in constructed Mikvaos. In order for a constructed Mikvah to be *Kosher* / effectively configured, it must be a gathering of rainwater. The 'natural' state of gathered rainwater is *Ash-Boren* / stationary, and not *Zochalin* / running, or flowing, as mentioned above. The waters of the Mikvah cannot be 'unnatural', such as tap-water, filtered water, or rainwater that was pumped or carried into the Mikveh by means of a vessel. In other words, the Mikvah cannot be *Sha'uvim* / 'drawn' by any human or mechanical intervention. "Just as springwater is natural (created by Heaven) the same is with a Mikvah (it is not pumped or carried water)…and just as a spring is in the ground, so too a Mikvah should be in the ground (not in a vessel)" (*Toras Kohanim*, Shemini, 11:36. Rashi, ibid).

Theoretically, the best possible rainwater Mikvah would be a simple pit in the earth. This is because any *Kli* / vessel that can be disconnected from the ground or is otherwise movable renders the water collected in it unkosher for a Mikvah. Ideally, natural rains would fill this pit over time, though there would of course be a technical problem of cleanliness if the pit were muddy. For instance, if you were to gather 40 Sa'ah of rainwater in your backyard by simply digging a large hole in the earth, even if you lined the hole with some non-removable water-repellent material, perhaps for your first few immersions the water would be clean. With repeated use, however, the water would become too dirty and perhaps even toxic, rendering the Mikvah unfit for use. For these reasons, today, Mikvah construction includes two pools. The one that you enter may be lined with tiles like a swimming pool. A second pool, which cannot see or enter, is constructed either underneath or to the side of the first one. This second pool is the 'real' Mikvah and contains rainwater that was funneled (not 'drawn', pumped or carried) from the top of the building. This same rainwater can stay in the concealed pool for years. The first pool has a hole a few inches in diameter, wide enough to comfortably rotate two fingers. This opening allows for the two waters to not only connect, but to actually 'become one', as explored by the Poskim (See *Aruch haShulchan*, Yoreh De'ah, 201:175-178).

This point of connection is called *Hashakah* / kissing, since through this hole the two waters 'kiss' and mingle. By means of this, the first pool becomes a Kosher Mikvah; you may therefore immerse in the first pool, even though it is filled with filtered tap-water. Due to the mingling and merging of these two waters, it is as if you are actually immersing in the natural rainwater of the second *Bor* / reservoir.

In summary, a Mikvah is a gathered body of rain (or spring water), that contains at least forty Sa'ah of water. When these basic conditions are met, a Mikvah is considered operational.

CHAPTER 2

~~~

Who Uses a Mikvah:
Tumah/Impurity & *Teharah*/Purity

On the most essential level, a Mikvah is used to transform a person or object from one status and state to another. (In this book we will be focusing almost exclusively on Mikvah immersion in relation to people, rather than objects.*) The Torah tells us that a person who is *Tamei* / in a state of ritual impurity, needs to immerse him or herself in a Mikvah to attain a state of *Teharah* / purity. *Tumah* is a noun, meaning 'ritual impurity'. A person or object that contracts Tumah is called by the adjective *Tamei* / impure.

It is crucial to understand that Tumah has nothing to do with physical hygiene or cleanliness, and of course that the Mikvah is not a 'bath'. In fact, one must be completely clean before entering into the Mikvah waters. Tumah is a ritual and spiritual state. This may or may not manifest as energetic, emotional or psychological imbalances or misalignments. Different from a regular 'bath', a Mikvah purifies us on an internal level for the purpose of spiritual elevation and intimacy.

---

* Our Sages also tell us that we even need to immerse new vessels that are purchased (not borrowed) from a non-Jew (*Avodah Zarah*, 75b). From Rashi (Zuza, ibid) it appears that is a *Gezeiras haKasuv* / a biblical decree, and not connected to any form of *Isur* / prohibited foods, meaning non-Kosher foods ingrained into the vessels, as these are new, unused vessels. And from *Tosefos* (Mag'ilan) it seems clear that this immersion has nothing to do with *Tumah* / impurity. Yet, the *Ritvah* (ad loc) brings from the Yerushalmi, that it does in fact have to do with Tumah; the vessels are leaving the domain of Tumah and entering the Kedushah of Klal Yisrael. The *Meiri* writes the same as the *Ritvah*.

There are various degrees of Tumah. The 'harshest' or most intense form of Tumah, called the *Avi Avos* / grandfather of all Tumah, occurs as a result of *Tumas Meis* / impurity of a corpse — when a living person touches a human corpse. All other forms of Tumah are called *Toldos* / offspring, as they are all in some way rooted in and subordinate to this primary Tumah of contact with death, as we will explore further.

The most closely related secondary categories of Tumah include circumstances such as standing in a building or roofed structure that contains a dead body, or coming into contact with certain dead insects. Today, these specific forms of Tumah have little practical impact. This is because the concept of Tumah is directly related to the *Beis haMikdash* / Holy Temple. If one was in a state of Tumah, they were prohibited from entering the Temple or participating in certain of its ritual functions. As there is presently no Beis haMikdash (may it be rebuilt soon, in our lifetime), and thus no access to certain purifying rituals that were performed there (e.g. the Red Heifer), there is no full remedy for Tumas Meis. Thus, it is assumed that we are all Tamei on a certain level, for over time most people will have come into contact with these types of Tumah. (Because a person who is Tamei for reasons other than contact with the dead can go to the Mikvah at the appropriate time, as we will explore, their Tumah could be considered (*Zevachim*, 108a) as less intense than those that cannot ever be *Metaher* / purified without the Temple.)

However, during the Temple period, when the Beis haMikdash stood, people who had come into contact with the dead were required to immerse in a Mikvah after a prescribed period of time before they could enter the Beis haMikdash or its vicinity. The Mikvah was thus the primary means for one to rejoin the sacred community following a period of prescribed distance.

Even today, there are still certain situations that require, according to Torah law, immersion in a Mikvah. For instance, the Torah, as revealed in its Oral Transmission, guides a woman to immerse in a Mikvah seven days after her monthly period as well as following the birth of a child, before she can return to intimacy with her husband.

A *Ger* / convert is another example of one who is required to immerse in a Mikvah. According to Torah law, one who has received upon himself the responsibility of Torah and keeping the Mitzvos — and if male, has had a *Bris* / ritual circumcision — is not considered fully converted until they immerse in a Mikvah. This is similar to Klal Yisrael, who, once they had left Egypt, had to immerse themselves in the waters that flowed from Sinai, prior to receiving the Torah at Sinai (*Yevamos*, 46a-b).

The prophet and scribe Ezra, who returned from the Babylonian exile and was instrumental in the building of the Second Beis haMikdash, established that all married men should immerse themselves in the Mikvah after being phys-ically intimate with their wives or releasing seed. This edict was not fully accepted by the entire congregation of Klal Yisrael and thus is not absolutely binding, although, even today, there are those who are careful to perform this im-mersion.* Even though it is not the law, this immersion will certainly help a person with their *Tefilah* / prayers, (*Or'chos Chayim*, 71. *Meiri*, Berachos, 221a), and as a result one's Tefilah will be more effective and accepted on High (*Talmidei Rabbe-inu Yonah*, on the Rif, *Berachos*, 13b).

There is also a very serious custom of Mikvah immersion *Erev* / the day before Yom Kippur (*Rosh*, Yuma, 8:24. *Shibbolei haLeket* 283. *Manhig*, 52. *Tosefos*, Berachos, 22b. *Tur*, *Mechaber*, Orach Chayim, 606:4). So important is this immersion that R. Saa-

---

* Ezra the Scribe decreed that men who are impure due to released seed cannot learn Torah before they immerse themselves (*Baba Kamah*, 82a). Later on, this edict was extended to *Tefilah* / praying as well (Rambam, *Hilchos Tefilah*, 4:4). "These decrees were not put into effect because of questions of ritual purity and impurity, but rather to ensure that Torah scholars would not overindulge in marital intimacy with their wives" (Rambam, ibid). Yet, since this was not fully accepted by all (and since it caused people to not learn Torah), the decree was abolished (Ram-bam, ibid, 4:5, and many other Rishonim: the Rosh, Rashba and Bahag. And such is the law: see *Shulchan Aruch haRav*, Orach Chayim, 88:1). Nevertheless, the Rambam himself always immersed himself (*Talmidei Rabbeinu Yonah* on the Rif, *Berachos*, 13b). The Rambam wrote (*Reishis Chochmah*, Sha'ar haAhavah, 11) that he always immersed for *Keri* / the release of seed, but he could not write as such in his book of Halacha, as it is not a law, but rather a personal custom. It is also possible that what was abolished is only the Mikvah immersion for learning Torah, not the Mikvah to pray. *Reishis Chochmah, ibid. Tosefos*, Berachos, 22b.

diah Gaon (882-942), the great leader and sage, suggests (although, this is not the law) reciting a *Beracha* / blessing on this immersion (*Rosh* and *Shibbolei haLeket*, ibid). Similarly, on any Erev Yom Tov, the day before a holiday, even today, it is strongly encouraged to immerse in a Mikvah.*

Further on in the text, more opportunities for immersing in the Mikvah such as on Erev Shabbos and various other occasions will be more deeply explored. For now, in order to develop a foundational understanding of Mikvah, we will focus on the three typologies mentioned above: a woman post-menstruation or post-birth, a convert, and a male after the release of seed. These three times of immersion are each a response to a specific form of Tumah, and the Mikvah allows a person in such a state to ritually transform them-

---

* "A person should purify himself before the *Regel* / holiday" *Rosh Hasha-nah*, 16b. The language of *Chazal* / our Sages is before the 'Regel', not the usual word, before Yom Tov. Why? *Regel* in numeric value is 233. This teaches us, says the Arizal, that when we immerse in the Mikvah on Erev Yom Tov we should have intention on the Name of Hashem that equal 233. This Name is a combination of Havayah and Ehe'yeh in their *Milu'im / filled-out* spellings: The Four Letter Name is spelled out as: **Yud** (Yud/10 + Vav/6 + Dalet/4 = 20), **Hei** (Hei/5 + Yud/10 = 15), **Vav** (Vav/6 + Yud/10 + Vav/6 = 22), **Hei** (Hei/5 + Yud/10 = 15), totaling 72. The Name *Ehe'yeh* is spelled out as **Aleph** (Aleph/1 + Lamed/30 + Pei/80 = 111), **Hei** (Hei/5 + Yud/10 = 15), **Yud** (Yud 10 + Vav/6 + Dalet/4 = 20), **Hei** (Hei 5 + Yud/10 = 15), totaling 161. When both names are added together the grand total (72 + 161) is 233 (*Sha'ar haKavanos*, Kavanos haTevilah Erev Yom Tov, p. 78a. *Kanfei Yonah*, Sod haTevilah. Shaloh, *Sha'ar haOsyos*, Kedushah, 8). Through-out the course of this text these Names will be further explored and explained, and thus their integral relevance to Mikvah immersions will become clear.

selves in order to reach *Teharah* / purity and a deeper form of *Kedushah* / holiness.*

However, before going any deeper into these three specific uses of the Mikvah, we need to address something much more fundamental that will allow us to grasp the root of what all these cases have in common. We must simply ask: What is Tumah and Teharah?

What is Tumah & Teharah?

As mentioned, the *Avi Avos* / grandfather of all Tumah comes from contact with a corpse, and all other forms of Tumah are considered *Toldos* / offspring. This suggests that the 'root' and deepest cause of all forms of Tumah is connection to some form of death, and what death represents.

---

* A Nidah is not only *Asur* / forbidden to have relations with her husband, but there is also a form of Tumah connected to a Nidah (*Sichos Kodesh*, 19th of Kislev, 1955. R. Yoseph Engel, *Asvan D'oiraisa*, 21 concludes that there is only *Isur* / prohibition. *Kuzari* Ma'amer 3:49. See also, *Noda b'Yehudah*, Tanina, Yoreh De'ah, 120. *Avnei Nezer* 2, 240). Perhaps, in reverse, even the Isur is derived from the Tumah (R. Elchanan, *Kovetz Shiurim* 2, Siman 43), and through the Mikvah, the Tumah and the Isur departs. (Mikvah can, apparently, also release the Isur itself, *Zevachim*, 43b.) A convert, through the immersion, is coming into a higher form of purity, and the Tumah connected to the Snake and the Garden of Eden is overtly released (*Shabbos*, 146a). The same applies to the male moving out of Tumah and entering Teharah.

The meta-root of death is the eating from the Tree of Knowledge of Good and Evil. All death and endings, separations and disconnections, fears and anxieties, entered the world through our eating from the Tree of Knowledge.

Meta-root of Death

Let us travel back in time to the first story of humans in the Torah. Adam and Chavah / Eve are created and they are living in Paradise according to the Tree of Life reality, in a state of total Oneness with Hashem, with themselves and with the world around them. There is no shame and no sense of separation. Then Hashem tells them, "From every tree of the Garden you may eat, but from the Tree of the Knowledge of Good and Evil you must not eat…." (*Bereishis*, 2:16-17).

Think about this for a moment: Adam and Chavah are living in the reality of the Tree of Life, in Paradise where there is no duality or opposites, no inside and outside, and no death, and yet they are told that they should not eat from the Tree of Good and Evil, the tree of duality. What's going on here? This is the simple, normative reading: there are two separate trees and paradigms, and they are told to choose one, and refrain from the other. Upon reflection however, this statement seems contradictory; if they could eat "of *every* tree", as the verse says, how can the second part of the statement say, "but from the Tree of the Knowledge of Good and Evil you must not eat"?

Based on this logical inconsistency, another way to read this narrative is that there is actually only 'one tree', one all-inclusive reality (*Pri Tzadik,* Tu b'Shevat). Hashem is therefore telling them, 'You may eat freely from *every tree* — alluding to the all-inclusive Tree of Life — but do not eat from any one specific, *separate* tree, to the exclusion of other trees, because then you will be entering the paradigm of the Tree of Duality' (*Maor vaShemesh,* Parshas Bo). That is, you may eat 'everything', just not 'something'. Meaning that, if you eat from every tree equally and do not make any exclusive distinctions, all will feel and taste the same. Even the non-fruit parts of the tree will then taste like fruit (*Medrash Rabbah,* Bereishis, 5:9). This is the Tree of Life paradigm, the way Adam and Chavah — and all of us — lived in the Garden of Eden at the inception of our creation.

What happened instead was that ותקח מפריו / "she took from its fruit" (*Bereishis,* 3:6). As the text indicates, they ate specifically *me'Piryo* / 'from' its fruit; the letter Mem in the beginning of the word means 'from', suggesting a separation. In other words, they judged and distinguished the fruit from other fruits, and separated the fruit from the tree, and thus entered the world of duality and separation. In a comment on this particular verse, the Zohar says that since they ate *mePiryo*, the Mem became dominant and they entered the world of *Maves* / Death, the world of judgment and separation (which begins with a Mem). As a result, death entered the world, along with the often devastating 'separation' from life as we know it.

In the world of the Tree of Life, there is no duality, separation or death. The decision made by Adam and Chavah in the Garden is also our decision whether or not to create and recreate a world of duality, a world of inside versus outside, of eternal life versus an end of life. Death, and the Tumah that comes along with it, are thus the results of choices made by Adam and Chavah, and are further perpetuated by our own choices from day to day, and even moment to moment. When we 'eat' or internalize anything *'from* the fruit' — taking something and rejecting other things, we are connecting to the world of death and Tumah, rather than life and purity.

In general, all negative actions and sins are in the paradigm of Tumah. The Torah itself calls each of the three most serious sins "a Tumah" (*Shavuos*, 7b). As a principle, this teaches us about all kinds of negativity. Every negative action, word or thought that we entertain potentially separates us from our own deepest selves, from others, and from the Source of All Life. All negative actions thus create a condition of 'death', often felt as a sense of *Yei'ush* / hopelessness, lack of enthusiasm, deadening of spirit or heaviness in the body.

Our Sages tell us (*Gittin*, 70a) that transgression is one of the things that diminish a person's *Koach* / strength, stamina and vitality, as the Pasuk in Tehilim says, "My *strength fails* because of my sin" (*Tehilim*, 31:11). King David also says, "For my iniquities have overwhelmed me; they are like a *heavy burden*, more than I can bear" (*Tehilim*, 38:5).

In other words, Tumah not only brings upon a person spiritual, mental and emotional heaviness and exhaustion, but heaviness and lethargy seeps into the body as well. Rabbi Yehudah haLevi (c. 1075-1141) tells us (*Kuzari*, Ma'amar 2:60) that a sensitive person who needs to immerse in a Mikvah but does not do so will actually feel heavy from the Tumah; the Tumah will physically weigh him down (see *Kol Yehudah*, ad loc). Tumah thus creates a deadness and an existential heaviness that has an effect on the body; the body becomes lethargic and heavy, with no *Koach* / strength.*

When we immerse in water, the burden of our physical weight is temporarily relieved. This is a physical representation of the inner impact of the Mikvah.

Additionally, the fluidity and movement of the water is a tangible experience of our inner return to flexibility and the ability to change.

---

* The *Mordechai* (*Chulin*, in the first chapter) writes this in the name of *Hilchos Eretz Yisrael* (Eldad ben Machli Hadani. *Tosefos* also quotes this Sefer in the beginning of Chulin regarding women and Shechita, see *Ramah*, Yoreh De'ah, 1:1), to stress that a Shochet must be sure to go to the Mikvah after *Keri* / bodily omission. Perhaps this is because before the Mikvah, a Shochet literally has less Koach, his body is heavy, and heaviness of the body is a reason not to perform Shechita (*Taz*, Yoreh De'ah, 1:18, regarding a drunk). The *Mordechai* (*Chulin* 571), citing the same Hilchos Eretz Yisrael, disqualifies a Shochet over 80 years old (or younger than 18), because he literally has less Koach.

The physical cleansing experience of immersion in water is a reflection of the inner cleansing of Tumah and any ego attachments to negative actions or aspects of our personality. When we perform the Mitzvah of Mikvah we become vividly lighter, unburdened of heavy thoughts and emotions. We emerge feeling more alive, invigorated and refreshed.

Tumah / Impurity and the Beis haMikdash

All Tumah is connected to a severance, an ending, a literal or metaphorical form of death. A person becomes *Tamei* / impure when he or she is in close contact with death or what death represents. As mentioned previously, the basic outcome of being Tamei is not being allowed to enter the spiritual center of society, the Beis haMikdash.

The Mishkan, the temporary temple in the Desert, was in the middle, the center of the encampment of the tribes. One who was Tamei could not enter into that space, and one who experienced a more intense form of Tumah was not even allowed to enter the outer court of the Temple. A person could, technically, walk through much of life in a state of Tumah, but he would be forbidden to enter the Mishkan and to participate in its sacred services.

Notably, the Beis haMikdash is also called *Beis Chayeinu* / The House of Our Life, and is the metaphysical node through which all life and renewal of life flows. When a person cuts himself off from *Elokim Chayim* / the Living Divinity, he enters the world of separation: separation within himself, between his body's needs and his soul's needs, between himself and others. Having severed himself from the integrity and flow of life itself, he is Tamei and is unable to enter the reality of *Beis Chayeinu*.

When the physical Temple stood proud in Yerushalayim / Jerusalem, it was the "eye of the world", the center of time, space and consciousness. It was the focal point of all Creation, the center from which all space flowed (*Yuma*, 54b. *Medrash Tanchuma*, Pikudei), and from which everything was birthed. There was a constant, palpable sense of newness and freshness there. The *Lechem haPanim* / showbreads never grew stale; they always tasted fresh, even if baked a week before (*Chagigah*, 26b). It is the archetypal/ultimate space of life, vitality, movement and freshness.

Parenthetically, there was a principle in the Beis haMikdash, that anyone who had relieved himself of feces was required to enter a Mikvah before he could resume his service there (Mishna, *Yuma*, 2:3. *Menachos*, 100a). This is because feces contain bacteria and dead epithelial cells from the lining of the gut that the body must eject. Feces is therefore a form of death, especially in relation to a place of extreme aliveness such as the Beis haMikdash.

It is relevant to note that the Temple was built on the site where Yaakov once slept and dreamt of a ladder connecting Heaven and Earth. When he awoke from this dream, he proclaimed, "Surely Hashem is in this place and I knew it not." What troubled him specifically was that he had slept in this holy place. Why? Our Sages call sleep "one sixtieth of death" (*Berachos*, 57b). Sleep is static, stagnant, and involves a certain level of Tumah (which is why we are instructed to wash our hands upon waking each morning). A holy place is alive, awake and bristling with alacrity, flow and movement. Yaakov was troubled that he did not tune into the resident energy of such a holy place, and that he was *able* to sleep there at all.

Notwithstanding the fact that there is currently no Holy Temple in Jerusalem, the spiritual dynamic of Tumah and Teharah that was played out during the period of the Beis haMikdash is still real today. When we cleave to Hashem and we are *Davuk* / one with Hashem, then *Chayim Kulchem haYom* / You are all alive today (*Devarim*, 4:4). In such a state we are viscerally connected to unity and life, in a tangible state of Teharah. When we disconnect ourselves from the Source of *Chayeinu* / our life, Heaven forbid, we are in a tangible state of Tumah — there is no more growth, movement or 'possibility'. By definition, everything disconnected from the Source of Life is dead, stationary, fixed and lifeless.

Pure, Revealed, Illuminated, Transparent

On an even deeper level, טהור / *Tahor* means more than 'pure'; it is also 'revealed' (see *Yuma*, 58b-59a, where the Sages call the *revealed* place within the Altar, *Taharah* / illuminating and brilliant. *Likutei Torah*, Yom Kipur, p. 69a). *Tahor* connotes clarity and transparency, as the *Pasuk* / verse says "וכעצם השמים לטהור / like the appearance of the Heavens for clarity" (*Shemos*, 24:10).

Tahor is also related to the word צהר / *Tzohar* / brilliant, illuminated, as Noach is told that "A *Tzohar* / *window* you shall make for the *Teiva* / Ark". This verse is interpreted as meaning that Noach should make a skylight, or affix a brilliant stone, to illuminate the Ark. So *Tahor* also alludes to a window opening to the outside, suggesting transparency and illumination. Indeed, in the language of our Sages, *Tahor* is used specifically in reference to light and day; for instance, when they speak about the presence of moonlight during the day, they refer to it as a שרגא בטיהרא / *Sh'raga b'Tiharah* / a candle in the daylight (*Chulin*, 60b).

By contrast, the word *Tumah* comes from the word *Sasum*, closed off, as in the word *Timtum* / shut off (*Yuma*, 39a). The root letters of *Tumah* are Tes-Mem. These two letters in sequence suggest something that is hidden, as in *Tamun* / concealed, *Hatmanah* / burial, or *Tumtum* / a person whose gender is concealed. Tumah is thus a concealment, a closing off. In the language of the Zohar, "A foreign (negative) force is hidden and does not bear fruit" (*Zohar* 2, 103a). In the state of Tumah we experience unyielding rigidity, suffering, the stunting of progress, and the closing off of productivity and fruition.

Tamei is spelled with a Tes, a Mem, and a silent Aleph. This suggests that to become Tamei is to enter a realm that is cut off, concealed — *Tes Mem* / separated from the *Aleph* / the One, the Master and Creator of the World (*Sefas Emes*, Shemini, 645). In other words, Tumah is when a person lives in a state of concealment, separation, stuckness, 'darkness' and a general deadness to purity, light and true life.

"The wicked are called dead" (*Berachos*, 18b). A 'dead' person rigidly holds onto grudges, is hardened into a posture of non-forgiveness, is trapped in a closed mental box, and buried in egoic reactivity. He is stuck in the past, holding on to old survival strategies, and unavailable to new perspectives. His body and mind are filled with suppressed anger, which can suddenly erupt against others and against life itself. From this constricted place, life is ultimately related to like an enemy.

Death and Tumah are often associated with the element of earth, whereas Teharah and life and the Source of Life are often associated with the element of water. As an example of this, our Sages teach that water nullifies all forms of *Kishuf* / black magic and demonic forces, however these may be understood (*Sanhedrin*, 67b. See also, *Zohar* 2, 82b). Earth is hard and inflexible, while water is soft and free of any fixed form, able to adapt to the shape of the container or context in which it is placed.

At its root, *Kedushah* / 'holiness' or purity, is aliveness. In such a state of vitality we enjoy lucidity, fluidity, movement, growth and productivity. Being connected to the Source of Life, we too are soft, alive, yielding and perpetually adaptable. A truly alive person is 'un-stuck', open, illuminating, and transparent.

Shedding Earth to be More like Water

As mentioned, earth is intimately related to death; both are lifeless, immobile and stationary. Death is also a return to earth. "You are earth and you will return to earth" (*Bereishis*, 3:19), or, as we say in our prayers on the High Holidays, "The foundation of man is from dust and his end is dust." Our bodies are from the earth, and since they are 'earth', we gravitate and are pulled towards the earth, towards the 'source' of the body. This is the natural state of the body: gravitating toward the earth.

Earth is inanimate, lacking in the qualities of revealed movement and vitality. It does not overtly expand like vegetation, nor move about like living animals. There is no animate life in earth itself. This is one dimension of our being, yet, it is not our entire makeup. Mixed into the earthy, inert body, there is water. As we noted, about 70 percent of the human body is made up of water — and as "man is a small world" and the entire world is called a "big man", about 70 percent of the earth's surface is covered in water as well. From one perspective, the body is earth, and from another the body is basically water.

Another characteristic of the element of earth is that each grain of sand is separate and distinct, so much so, that when a wind comes, it blows sand into all different directions. Yet, when the element of water is added, the individual grains of sand become unified. You cannot build a sandcastle or mud hut without the binding agent of water. Water unifies and solidifies earth. So it is with the body. Conceptually, the water of the body unifies the earth of the body, keeps it together as a unit, and ensures its health and integration. The earth element of the body represents that which is *Gashmi* / physical, tangible, and lifeless, and the water element of the body represents the more fluid, spiritual, primordial, life-giving element within the body.

Death occurs when the *Chayus* / life force or water of the body departs. Then, indeed, dust returns to the dust: "The dust returns to the ground it came from, and the Spirit returns to G-d who gave it" (*Koheles*, 12:7).

Every form of Tumah and Nidah contains a trace of this severance of 'earth' and 'water', cutting one off from vitality, hope, movement and unity. To recalibrate the system and allow for the Chayus to once again pulsate throughout the body and consciousness, the body needs to immerse in the element of water. We take our body, which has had a brush with the world of separation and 'death', and we immerse it within מים חיים / *Mayim Chayim* / living waters, to revitalize and 'reunify' ourselves on all levels.

Transmitting vs. Receiving Tumah

Certain things transmit Tumah — anything connected to 'death' or what it represents. Certain objects (including people) can also be *Mekabel* / receiving, attracting and absorbing Tumah. For instance, in order for a fruit or a vessel to be Mekabel Tumah it must be a 'finished product'; it must be symbolically 'dead' in the sense of completed through the processing or intention of a freely choosing human being (*Meshech Chochmah*, Vayera). When something is done growing or forming and is thus ready to be eaten or ready to be used, it means it is no longer in a process of 'becoming', and it is conceptually/functionally dead.

Any food that people normally eat can absorb Tumah (*Uk-tzin*, 3:1). A fruit, for example, is able to be Mekabel Tumah when it is no longer attached to the tree. In the words of the Rambam, "So long as the fruit is attached, even with a small root, (enough) that it can get *Chayus* / life force… (it is) not Mekabel Tumah (*Hilchos Tumas Ochlin*, 2:1). Simply put, for a fruit to be Mekabel Tumah the fruit needs to be 'dead' and completely ready to be eaten; meaning, it is no longer connected to the tree that gave it life and stimulated growth. Similarly, for meat to be Mekabel Tumah, the animal needs to be dead, or, the piece must be a dead limb unable to be rejuvenated (*Ibid.*, 2:6).

In the example of a fruit separated from its source of life, there is another requirement needed for it to be susceptible to Tumah: it needs a *Hechsher* / preparation composed of water, or it needs to have come in contact with water or one of the seven liquids defined by our Sages (*Machshirin*, 6:1. Rambam, *Hilchos Tumas Ochlin*, 1:1). Specifically, this means that water that is 'detached' from the ground must fall upon the fruit with the approval of its owner, and only then can it be Mekabel Tumah.

The reason why an already ripe fruit needs this Hechsher and requires intentional contact with water in order to be Mekabel Tumah is because this act 'completes' the fruit, making it completely ready to be eaten. We can see this today when people wash a piece of fruit before eating it. This washing is thus considered the fruit's completion, making it finally ready to be eaten.

Yet, only water that is no longer 'alive', such as collected water from a vibrant stream or gathered rainwater, and water that is no longer attached to ground renders the fruit susceptible to Tumah (*Ibid.*, 2:8).

This category of water is the exact opposite of the water needed for a Mikvah. Purifying waters are connected to the earth, either springwater or rainwater, and not water that was gathered in a *Kli* / vessel. ("Just as a spring is in the ground, so too a Mikvah should be in the ground [not a vessel]" *Toras Kohanim,* Shemini, 11.) Therefore, the kind of water that is needed to 'complete' the fruit is water that has also 'died' as it were. From all the above, it is clear that for something to connect to and accept Tumah, it must already be in a condition of death. Tumah connects itself to something (someone) that is already susceptible to Tumah.

Regarding someone who is a *Metzorah* / ritually a leper, the Torah says that the Cohen who inspects the Metzorah וטמא טמא יקרא / "shall declare, unclean, unclean" (*Vayikra,* 13:45). The reason for this public declaration is so people should know to stay away (*Rashi,* Toras Kohanim, 13:155), and also to pray for him (*Moed Katan,* 5a). A more interpretive reading of these words is, "And to a Tamei, declare Tamei." Meaning, the reason he becomes Tamei and attracts Tumah is that he lives a life of Tumah, and ultimately Tumah attracts more Tumah (R. Moshe Dovid Valli, *Eis Lachenina,* 2, p. 61-62). We attract what we are. As our Sages phrase it, "Poverty follows the poor" (*Baba Kamah,* 92a-b). A Tamei tends to be Mekabel Tumah.

For a fruit, vessel or person to receive Tumah, they need to already be living in at least a subtle kind of Tumah, whether in mourning, separation, loss, death, stuckness, isolation, or a state of *Yei'ush* / giving up. Simply put: A human being attracts Tumah and can assimilate it within him or herself, because when a person touches a corpse, or is post-menstruation, post-birth, or post -emission their consciousness is connected to a state of 'death' or loss of life. Similarly, the transmitting object itself also needs to be hovering in the world of Tumah, fixity and death.

After having developed a deeper understanding of the nature of Tumah and Tehara, we can now return to our three basic types of people who need to immerse in a Mikvah, as mentioned above. Remember, these three cases are not the only reasons for immersing in a Mikvah, as we will explore later in the text. However, they do provide us with paradigmatic examples to deepen our general appreciation for the spiritual function and inner workings of the Mikvah.

Monthly Nidah

A Nidah is the first example of a person who, even in the present era, is required to immerse in a Mikvah. Keeping in mind that Tumah is connected to death, and all that death represents, as explained above, will help us more deeply understand the laws of Nidah and the effects of immersing in a Mikvah.

So, let's start at the beginning: who or what is a *Nidah*? A woman is considered a *Nidah* from the onset of her menstruation until she counts seven 'pure days' and immerses herself in a Mikvah (*Vayikra*, 15:19). The word נידה /*Nidah* comes from the root word נד /*Nad* / moved or removed. As during this time period spouses are 'removed' from physical intimacy. These laws are derived from the following Torah verse: "A woman with whom a man cohabited, whereby there was [a discharge of] semen, they shall immerse in water" (*Vayikra*, 15:18). This verse refers specifically to a woman who was intimate with her husband and therefore not a Nidah, however we learn: "This teaches a general principle with regard to any impure person, they are in a state of impurity until they immerse" (Rambam, *Hilchos Issurei Biah*, 4:3. This teaching originates from the Geonim. *Rabbeinu Bachya*, ibid). Although the specific obligation for a Nidah to immerse in a Mikvah is only revealed later in the Oral aspect of Torah, we do find an earlier allusion in the Book of Zecharyah: "On that day, a spring shall be opened for the house of David and for the inhabitants of Jerusalem, for purification and for sprinkling and for the Nidah" (*Zecharyah*, 13:1). But, why does menstruation render a woman Tamei?

Menstruation is a subtle form of death, the loss of a potential life. Every month, the body of a fertile female releases an internal egg, which if fertilized with sperm, may become an embryo. The uterus, which holds the egg, fills with blood during the time the egg is released, in order to help nourish the egg. If fertilization does not occur, the egg, together with the extra build-up of blood, is expelled from the body, and this is the monthly menstrual 'bleeding'. Nidah is thus rooted in the loss of the potential fertilization of the egg, as well as the release of the excess blood that will not be used to protect newly created life. This flow of blood causes the status of Nidah.

The womb which holds the embryo, allows it to become a fetus, and finally births new life, is called in Hebrew: *Rechem*. The word *Rechem* has three Hebrew letters: Reish, Ches, Mem. These three letters read backwards as *Machar* / tomorrow. The womb is the embodied possibility of a tomorrow, a future. This is the feminine power to perceive (and produce) the future, to know the possibility of becoming, the promise of being freed from past and present conditions.

When a female body releases menstrual blood it represents the death or ending of a specific possibility of new birth, the closing of a specific 'tomorrow', and thus it is an experience of Tumah.

Parenthetically, *Rechem* and *Machar* are both numerically 248, representing the *RaMaCh* / 248 positive Mitzvos of the Torah. The Torah is life: it is the *Eitz haChayim* / Tree of Life, the *Toras Chayim* / the Torah of Life. Through immersing in the Torah, which is likened to water, we connect to the Source of All Life. As a result, we are not stuck in the 'today', in current appearances, but alive with a dream and aspiration for a brighter future.

Having come into contact with the 'death' of potential life, and having thus become Tamei (*Tamei'ah* in the feminine), the way a woman will rejoin the world of life, movement, hope and possibility, is through immersion in a Mikvah. It should now be clear that immersion in a Mikvah is not about becoming 'clean', but rather about becoming alive again.

Nidah through Childbirth

When life is successfully brought into existence, there is paradoxically an experience of 'death' at the same time. Rabbeinu Bachya (Spain, 1255-1340) writes, "A child, from the moment of birth, begins to dry up." From the moment of birth there is introduced a potential, and an inevitability, of death. This is perhaps a reason for postpartum Tumah. Yet, if this is so, it would seem that the child would be rendered Tamei, not the mother. The question is then, why does the mother become a Nidah, a Tamei'ah?

It can be argued that the mother becomes Tamei'ah because the process of childbirth is by nature life-threatening. Until quite recently the mortality rate in childbirth was quite high. According to this view, as the mother encounters the shadow of death, she is energetically impacted, and becomes ritually impure. However, from a deeper psychological perspective, it can be said that birth itself is intimately related to death. How so?

No beginning ensues without marking an end to something else. Every birth is concurrent with the 'death' or end of another form or stage of life. For the duration of the pregnancy, the mother may feel one with the fetus. With the dramatic event of birth, all of a sudden this form of unified life ceases and the child is separate from the mother. She may thus have ambivalent feelings related to the experience of birth. This may in fact be part of the phenomenon of postpartum depression, which could be seen as a psycho-physical expression of 'Tumah'.

In Halacha, a man is called a father at the moment the mother conceives a child, whereas the mother is not considered a mother until she gives birth. From the perspective of the father, the moment there is a child in the womb he has fathered a separate being that is now residing within his wife's womb. From the mother's perspective, the child within her is not an independent, separate being. Prior to birth, the child is technically considered the *Yerech* / 'limb' of the mother according to all opinions, as the child exists and lives only within the mother (R. Yoseph Engel, *Beis haOtzer*, Av. Maharal, *Ohr Chadash*).

Whereas birth is the 'beginning of life' for the child, for the mother, there is an experience of 'death'. (Thus, only once the fetus is initially formed as a 'human child' is the mother Tamei through birth. R. Meir argues that in all situations the mother is Tamei at birth. See *Nidah*, 23b, *Tosefos, ad loc.*, *Rashi* and the *Rambam* on Vayikra, 12:1.) Throughout the pregnancy, the mother is one with the fetus, constituting a single living being. When the baby emerges as an individual being, the cord is cut and there is an intense separation. This separation sharply marks the mother's 'death' of her previous experience of total union with the child, and she thereby enters a state of Tumah.

Similar to the seven clean days after menstruation, when post-birth bleeding stops, the Tamei'ah woman waits seven clean days after giving birth and then she can immerse herself in the Mikvah. These seven days also mirror the seven days of *Shivah* / mourning for a close relative. They allow her time to grieve for losing the feeling of her child within her own body. And like the laws of Shivah, by which the mourner is allowed to be quiet and to not engage in conversation, during these seven days the woman has a quiet time, and does not engage in intimacy with her husband.*

---

* In Torah law, for the birth of a male there is a seven day period of Tumah, and for the birth of a female a 14 day period. Perhaps this is because there is a 'double' state of mourning for the birth of a female, since the baby girl will also, G-d willing, give birth (at birth, a baby girl's ovaries already contain all of the eggs of her future children), and thus within the woman's body there had been two 'generations' of life. Interestingly, the word *Zachar* / boy starts with the letter Zayin which is the seventh letter of the Aleph-Beis, alluding to seven days of Tumah. *Nekeivah* / girl begins with the letter Nun, the 14th letter, alluding to the 14 days of Tumah. Rabbi Chayim ben Betzalel, brother of Maharal, *Igeres haTiyul*, Zayin.

Once the seven days are up, she immerses herself in a Mikvah and she is pure.

Convert

Just as the entire Klal Yisrael, when they left Egypt, needed to immerse themselves in a Mikvah before receiving the Torah at Mount Sinai, when a person goes through a conversion they also need to immerse their body in a Mikvah to receive the full transformation and transmission of their new status.

By eating — and identifying — with the Snake and the Tree of Knowledge, the human being became mortal; death became experienced as the 'opposite' of life. As should now be clear, death equals Tumah. Our Sages tell us that ever since Adam and Chavah listened to the snake, i.e. were 'intimate' with the snake, a spirit of *Zehumah* / impurity became attached to humanity. (Tumah is called *Zehumah* in the language of the Torah, *Resisei Layla*, 19.) When Klal Yisrael accepted the Torah of Life and Purity, this Zehuma left them. It also essentially left all future converts, as they too, on a deeper soul level, experienced the revelation at Mount Sinai (*Shabbos*, 156a. *Tosefos*, *Avodah Zarah*, 22b). On a practical, revealed level, however, when converts choose to connect with the *Toras Chayim* / Torah of Life, also known as the Tree of Life, they move into a higher state of Teharah, purity and life, and for this reason, the convert is required to immerse in a Mikvah.

On the one hand, a convert is someone who has a 'spark of a Jewish soul' even from birth. This is often manifest in a deep sense of connection to the Jewish people and to teachings of the Torah from a very young age. In the language of our Sages, a convert is a " גר שנתגייר /convert who converted" (*Yevamos*, 22a). This suggests that the convert is already converted, already 'Jewish' even before the actual conversion (*Shevilei Emunah*, Nosiv 3, p. 129. *Siddur R. Yaakov Emdin*, Leil Shabbos). Yet, when converts begin to live physically and openly as Halachic Jews, they receive and embody a higher level of soul. There is a unique source for the souls of converts (*Sha'ar haGilgulim*, Hakdamah 12, 13), and once they convert, they receive spiritual influx from this source and it can become manifest within them as an even higher level of soul (*Sha'ar haGilgulim*, Hakdamah 34). This movement and reception of the higher soul demands a Mikvah immersion. The Mikvah thus allows for the shedding of the convert's old life, the *Bitul* / nullification of their previous *Yesh* / existence, so that a new, more luminous Yesh can be revealed (a convert is like someone who is "פורש מן הקבר / separates from the grave" Mishnah, *Pesachim*, 92b).

Men's Mikvah

There is another use of the Mikvah we will consider in the chapter, which was mandated by Ezra the Scribe, and that is for every male to immerse themselves in a Mikvah after intimacy and the release of semen. Today, this ruling is no longer accepted as binding upon all, but is still practiced by many.

Male seed has the potential of life. When it is released not for the purpose of creating life, it is considered 'wasted' life force, wasted potential. Furthermore, every time a man releases seed, there is a subtle form of death; in fact, thousands of potential lives technically exist within thousands of spermatozoa. Also, when the male releases seed, he is taking all the energy of his body, from the bottom of his toes to the crown of his head, and ejecting it from his body. Seed is the sum total of a person's *Koach* / bodily energy and thus when released, a tiredness sets in, as one has just given fully of his essence. Thus, this act of release should only be done with intention, attention, holiness, care, and in a state of true *Yichud* / unity and love with one's spouse. Certainly, it is not something to be taken lightly and mindlessly, G-d forbid. In any case, a minor form of death occurs every time a man releases seed, resulting in an emptying of vitality and essential life force from the body.

In fact, all bodily ejections, including even digestive waste, are expressions of Tumah — although not literally. Similar to how a Cohen is not allowed to become Tamei, and therefore cannot stand within four Amos (approximately six feet) of a corpse, Halacha requires everyone to distance themselves four Amos from (adult) feces before praying. Once a biological substance leaves the body, whether blood, semen or waste, it carries at least some degree of Tumah energy with it, as well as implies some form of loss or depletion for the body.

Hashem tells Adam and Chavah that "On the day that you eat from it (the Tree of Knowledge, Good and Evil) you are going to die." This did not mean that they would die then and there, rather that they would enter into a world of duality: good, evil and separation, and thus eventual death. In addition, this world of separation contains the phenomenon of waste, for example, not everything eaten can be integrated into the body, and not every seed bears fruit. Before eating from the Tree of Knowledge, the food of Adam and Chavah was like the *Mon* / manna in the Desert, the 'food of angels', and therefore it produced no waste. The Mon was "absorbed by all the 248 parts of the body and no refuse was left" (*Yuma*, 74b). Once they descended into the world of separation certain substances were absorbed into the body and others were separated and rejected as waste. Waste is the used up energy of the body, coupled with actual dead cells that the body expunges. Similarly, menstrual blood is the flushing of dead cells and unfertilized eggs.

In a different but related way, when a male releases the energy of his body, he is dying slightly, depleting himself of vitality as well as allowing potential life to die. For this reason, in order to recharge, refresh and rejuvenate his life force, he should immerse himself in a Mikvah and become *Tahor* /

pure, transparent and alive again. This is especially true before he learns Torah and prays, as both of these sacred acts seek to place him back into relationship and realignment with the Tree of Life and the Source of Life. He should thus cleanse himself of all vestiges of the Tree of Knowledge, as explored above.

By why does water specifically have the power to effect this existential shift in status and energy? In the next chapter, we will dive into the spiritual and physical makeup of water to more deeply understand its elemental nature and symbolic significance.

CHAPTER 3

The Nature of Water

BEFORE DELVING MORE DEEPLY INTO THE SPECIAL POWER OF THE MIKVAH, WE NEED to explore the spiritual nature of water, and how the Torah views the chemical formula of H_2O (a molecule that contains one oxygen and two hydrogen atoms): a molecule which is so integral to life, that it covers most of the earth's surface and comprises most of our body.

Water: The Root from which All of Creation Emerges

To understand the nature of water, we need to uncover meaning in the first time the Torah speaks of water. The root of every idea, object or invention in creation is the way it is explored in the Torah, and the deepest root of idea lies in its first mention. Therefore, to understand the nature of water, we need to investigate its first mention in the Torah. The Torah opens with the words, *Bereishis* / "In the (for a) beginning G-d created the Heavens and the Earth." Then it continues, "The earth was astonishingly empty, and darkness was on the face of the deep, and the spirit of G-d was hovering over the face of the *water*. And G-d said, "Let there be light" (*Bereishis*, 1:1-3). The first, specific and distinguished creation was *Ohr* / light, yet, according to the text, before light there was already water.

In Pirkei Avos we learn: "The world was created with ten utterances...(although, it could have) been created with

Ma'amar Echad / one utterance..." (*Avos*, 5:1). Hashem says *Yehi...* / "let there be..." nine times throughout the creation narrative. There are thus nine revealed declarations. What is the tenth utterance? According to the Sages, the word *Bereishis* is also a *Ma'amar* / utterance (*Rosh Hashanah*, 32a). The hidden, transcendent 'tenth' utterance, which is actually the first, or *Echad*, is thus the word *Bereishis* itself (*Maharsha*, ad loc. According to *Zohar* 3, 11b, and *Pirkei d'Rebbe Eliezer*, however, "Let there be light" is the Ma'amar Echad).

The difference between creation as it is articulated in the Ma'amar Echad and creation as it is generated through the nine utterances, is that with the Ma'amar Echad, all phenomena are spoken into existence as one undifferentiated unity. The singular state of creation sourced in the Ma'amar Echad is therefore connected to and expressive of the ultimate Oneness of the Creator.

With the Ma'amar Echad, all of Creation was created *b'Koach* / in potential (*Ramban*, Bereishis, 1:1. *Umunos v'De'os*, Ma'amar 31. *Moreh Nevuchim*, 2:26. *Derashos haRan*, 1). The Ma'amar Echad is representative of the *Ayin* / no-thing-ness that includes all the *Yesh* / something-ness in potential. And then, through the gradual revealing of the nine utterances and their infinite amount of combinations and permutations (*Tanya*, Sha'ar haYichud v'HaEmunah, 1), a world of apparent multiplicity and separation arose.

The nine utterances are the world as we know it, the world of distinctions — sun and moon, up and down, right and left, man and stone. The first of these utterances distinguished and separated out the phenomenon of light from the pre-existing darkness. It is appropriate that light was the first distinct creation, as light is what allows us to see and relate to all other distinctions.

Whereas light is the first 'revealed' utterance, even before the 'revelation' of light, water was, according to the Torah itself, already present. Water is thus rooted within the realm of the Ma'amar of *Echad* / Oneness.

That is not to say that water was not 'created'. Water is most certainly a creation, distinct from other creations, however the source of water is the Ma'amar Echad, which first created a world of total unity. This world of oneness still exists, although from our dualistic perspective it remains "hidden". Water is thus an expression of singularity, and has a unifying effect on whatever it touches.

Fire on the other hand is rooted in the *Ohr* / light of Creation, the second utterance. Fire can break apart objects that it comes in contact with, and it can also weld objects together. A booklet of paper that catches fire breaks into many tiny pieces of ash. If water were to soak into a booklet of paper, the booklet would stick together and become like one mass.

On a deeper level, the Ma'amar Echad is not only the 'first utterance', rather, it is the *Nekudah* / point of oneness that exists within all the other utterances. Water is the foundation of life and the inner quality upon which everything stands, as alluded to in the verse, "The land and the fullness thereof are Hashem's, the world and those who dwell therein, for He founded it upon seas" (*Tehilim*, 24:1-2). Within the world of the nine utterances of duality, there is a Nekudah of *Yichud* / unity deep within, like a drop or molecule of water, holding it together as a cohesive unit, in other words — a unity.

Water & Desire

Energetically, water is connected to *Ta'avah* / desire and pleasure (*Sha'arei Kedushah*, 1:1. *Tanya*, 1). Water is so deeply connected to desire, that the moment a physical desire is aroused, moisture naturally appears. For example, when a person has a desire for food, he salivates and moisture builds up in his mouth. Similarly, when humans, animals and other forms of life, have a desire to procreate, both מים נוקבין /*Mayim Nukvin* / feminine waters and מים דוכרין / *Mayim Duch'rin* / masculine waters begin to flow. Water is therefore not only metaphysically connected to desire, but physically as well. And yet, the microcosm is a reflection of the macrocosm: the meta-root of water is in Hashem's desire, a Divine desire to create, which is also called *Mayim Duch'rin.*

Hashem's desire to create is the deepest source and cause of all Creation. This desire gave voice to the Ma'amar Echad, the unifying 'water', which is the Nekudah of oneness and aliveness within every phenomenon.

There are various revealed 'reasons' as to 'why' the world was created. For example, since "The nature of the Good is to give goodness" (*Emek haMelech*, Sha'ar 1:1. *Derech Hashem. Da'as Tevunos*, 18. *K'lach Pischei Chochmah*, 3), the Source of Goodness created a world in order to bestow such goodness upon it. Another reason is that only a finite, multi-faceted, multi-dimensional Creation could "reveal the complete array and perfection of His powers and deeds"; in other words: the ultimate power of an Infinite Reality is to create and reveal finitude (*Eitz Chayim*, Sha'ar 1, Derush Igulim v'Yosher). Another reason offered for why we were created is "so that we should know the Creator" (*Zohar* 2, 42b), and acknowledge Hashem's existence (*Ramban*, Bo, 13:16).

However, the difficulties with all of these revealed 'reasons' are the following: a) if the Creator had just created angelic beings (i.e., with no freewill), they would have been sufficient recipients to satisfy the 'need' to bestow goodness. And not only would they be more appreciative of the Creator's power, they would certainly 'know Him' better, also satisfying that reason. Furthermore, b) any 'reason' given suggests a 'need' and need suggests a 'lack', something that is 'missing' that can be 'completed', and the Creator does not lack.

The angels' superior appreciation and capacity-to-know G-d is indeed a 'reason' that the upper worlds were created, but the question still remains: why was a lower world of time and space and human struggles created? The Alter Rebbe quotes the Medrash (*Tanchumah*, Naso, 16, see also, *Medrash Rabbah*, Bamidbar, 10) which states that the purpose of the entire Creation is to satisfy "Hashem's *desire* to have a *Dirah* / dwelling in the *Tachtonim* / lower realms" (*Tanya*, Chap. 36). There was simply a Divine *Ta'avah* / desire to create the world.

While this is presented as a 'reason', it is really beyond the paradigm of reason. Why? Because the nature of Ta'avah itself is beyond reason. As we know: "You cannot ask a question on a desire" (Rashab, *Yom Tov Shel Rosh Hashanah*, Samach Vav, p. 7. *Ohr haTorah*, Balak, p. 997. According to the Rambam, we cannot talk about an ultimate reason for Creation, as Hashem Himself is utterly unknowable, *Moreh Nevuchim*, 3:13). A desire is not a 'need', it is not a movement to complete something that is missing or lacking. Even in our world, people often have certain desires that are not rationally explainable or even justifiable. Hashem had a desire to dwell in the lower worlds. Why? You cannot ask questions on desire; Hashem just wanted it and there is no other reason.

Ta'avah, the innermost cause and foundation of Creation, is, as discussed, embodied within the quality of water. And for this reason, the first substance to be mentioned in the

Torah, beyond 'emptiness' and 'darkness', and after the very general categories of "Heaven and Earth", is water.

All of this means that the inner essence of Creation, its inner *Nekudah* / point, its omnipresent 'molecule', is the Divine desire to dwell here. All of nature is forever evolving to manifest this Divine desire, which is the engine that perpetually propels Creation to continue to exist and progress towards that ultimate indwelling.

Man is created in the Divine image. As such, the greatest manifestation of the Divine desire is encoded within the human being, and in his or her actual desires. All human desire is thus rooted in the Divine desire. As such, we ultimately have but one true desire: to fulfill the Divine desire. (Moshe hit the rock to receive water because he wanted to break human desire in order to attain Divine desire. However, Hashem wanted him to speak to the rock, and show that the deepest desire of the people is already Divine — the desire to connect with Hashem. R. Tzadok, *Resisei Layla*, Os 58.) Sometimes, people think they are desiring food, a new car, another person, or a new gadget, but on the deepest level, all they are desiring is to manifest the Divine desire of Creation, to connect with Hashem. They are merely misdirecting the energy of this sacred desire. Instead of focusing their awareness on *Yichud* / unity with Hashem, they divert it into Yichud with a new bag, person or gadget.

From this perspective we can see that desire itself, the want/ longing to be 'at one with', is pure and holy. The sensation of desire for Yichud has no 'form', rather it's an abstract want/yearning to reach out and connect. It is only the *narrative* superimposed upon the sensation, in particular the story we tell ourselves about who or what is going to satisfy a particular desire, which can direct it toward wastefulness or negativity.

As the archetypal expression of the Ma'amar Echad, water is the embodiment of the quality of desire for Yichud, the driving force of all life. Therefore, immersing in water has a visceral effect on us, as it transports us back into the state of Yichud from which we all came. It brings us back to the womb and root of Creation, as 'water within water', returning us to the primordial state of the world when the earth itself was completely submerged in water. The word מקוה / Mikvah contains the letters קו / line. By entering the Mikvah we enter a portal, line or path, which elevates us back into the womb of Creation, the place of ultimate Yichud where we realign our desires and reclaim our deepest, purest self. In the Mikvah we become filled again with קוה / hope, as we tap into the infinite possibility of restarting our life refreshed, renewed and recommitted to making our body and mind a dwelling for the Infinite One, thereby fulfilling Hashem's original divine desire at the root of all creation.

Water:
The Element with No Tzurah / Form or Color

Desire, on its own, is like water, having no *Tzurah* / form. There is no inherent narrative to desire, although for desire to be expressed outwardly it needs to be focused on a particular object of desire. This is similar to electricity; while electricity is everywhere, one does not observe it until it is harnessed to power a lightbulb or a toaster. Desire is pure, raw and generative energy. It only becomes detrimental for a person when its power is channeled into something, or someone, in particular that is not appropriate or healthy for them to acquire or engage with.

In our own lives, desire ensures that we get up in the morning, get out of bed, and do something with our lives. Some people have a burning desire to learn Torah, some to pray and connect with Hashem or their community, and some to make money or be famous. Some simply desire to be good honest people, good husbands or wives, children, friends or parents. This is not a hierarchy of values, rather, it is just to point out that whatever your deeper desires are is what compels you to act in the world. Just as Divine desire inspires an action within Hashem, so to speak, a 'movement' to create a world of time and space out of infinite unity, so it is with every created being. Desire is what moves us and all living beings to survive, procreate, develop, acquire, engage and expand.

Desire moves us to connect with something or someone outside of ourselves, much like Divine desire moves the Creator to create and connect with Creation. In the simplest terms, desire connects and unites. It is the link/bridge between us and the world around us. But on its own, desire itself has no 'form', it is not particular and contextualized; it can be expressed as a desire that connects us to money, or a desire that connects us to other people or a desire to sense our intimate closeness with Hashem.

Water, just like the quality of desire that it represents, also has no 'shape' or Tzurah (Maharal, *Gevuras Hashem*, 18). Additionally, as water is rooted in the infinite Divine desire of Hashem (Ma'amar Echad), it also has no particular identifying color (*Siddur Im Dach*, Kavanos Mikvah). Only when water is placed within a vessel does it take on a particular 'shape', as it were, and appear from the outside to have 'color'. Without any external imposition and definition, however, water is formless and colorless.

Running water is continually changing its Tzurah, depending on the contours and curvature of the area within which it is flowing. It is fluid, malleable and in a constant state of movement. The Torah therefore uses water as an image of restlessness, as in, "the restlessness of water" (*Bereishis*, 49:4). Water is dynamic; it is always seeking a course to move from a higher position to a lower plane (*Ta'anis*, 7a). With regards to a ship in the ocean, our Sages say, "The ship is steady, stationary, and it is the waters that are moving" (*Baba Metzi'a*, 9b. *Tosefos, Shabbos*, 5b). Water, in contrast to solid earth, is ceaselessly shifting, and thus if you lift an object floating on the water it is not considered as if you lifted an object from a specific, defined space (*Shabbos,* 5b, Rashash).

This quality of perpetual motion is also perhaps the reason (see *Gevuras Hashem*, 18) that water is normally referred to in the plural, *Mayim*, not *Mai*. The implied multiplicity of *Mayim* suggests that every individual drop of water is actually an integral part of the single comprehensive body of water that covers and courses throughout the entire world. It suggests a unification of multiple objects. So too, water, like desire, serves to connect and unify us with other subjects and objects of our desire outside of ourselves.

For two separate entities to become united, there must be something deep within both of them that is the same. For example, when two people marry each other, they can be joined "as one flesh" because, on a deep level, they are actually separate parts of a single soul. Similarly, two wet pieces of paper become forged together and unified because the water reveals their deeper shared qualities. In spiritual terms, the water reveals the Ma'amar Echad, the Divine desire that binds together the multiplicity of Creation, the shared point of unity in every phenomenon in which everything exists as part of a cosmic singularity.

Water is the 'Place' of Unity

Water is thus the point of Unity within all. Indeed, water is unity itself.

This realization will help us to better grasp the wonderful Mitzvah and practice of Mikvah. But before proceeding further, here is a short teaching from Rebbe Nochum of Chernobyl (1730-1797), an early Chassidic Rebbe, on one of the deep benefits of immersing in a Mikvah (*Maor Einayim*, Yismach Lev, 504):

"Mikvah means 'gathered', unified, as a Mikvah is the secret of the World of Unity (See also *Siddur Im Dach*, Kavanos Mikvah), connected to the World of Thought. Now, it is known that the main (capacity) of the human being is thought, and, 'The place where a person's thoughts are, that is where he is.' When a person's thoughts are scattered, jumping incoherently from one thought to the next, he is experiencing a dispersion of his *Nefesh* / lower level of soul. For the Nefesh is what brings vitality to a person's thought. When a person goes into the Mikvah, he enters into the world of Unity: a place where all his thoughts are gathered and unified. Prior to entering the Mikvah, he may have operated in the world of *Pirud* / separation, and thus a 'space' that allows for brokenness (hence the possibility for *Tumah* / negativity, impurity, separation, the concept of death). Now that he enters the waters of the Mikvah, which is the world of Unity, all is purified...."

When a person is committed to a higher purpose and is totally focused and 'gathered', then his thoughts are in line with who he truly is, and he has full control over his thoughts, emotions, words and actions. In this place, he is a 'unified' person, a *Tzadik*. He is an integrated person who is not helplessly and unconsciously reactive to others and to the world, but he is firmly rooted within his soul and within his truth, "like a tree planted by the water..." (*Yirmiyahu*, 17:8, or *Tehillim*, 1:3).

When we immerse ourselves in the waters of the Mikvah, we too become water-like and return to the world of Unity, from whence we come; we become gathered, focused and whole again.

~~~~~

CHAPTER 4

Immersion in Water

Tumah, as explored above, means much more than simply 'impure'. It is a type of energetic stuckness, rigidity, separation and even 'death', which is experienced as being fragmented, alienated, depressed, or without hope. This state can be brought on by a number of different circumstances which bring us into contact with the liminal zone between life or its opposite, including sleep, birth, loss of potential life, loss of vitality, or simply being close to the reality of death, as in touching or being in close proximity to a corpse. Now that we also have a working understanding of the nature of water, as discussed in the previous chapter, we can combine these insights to understand more deeply why a Mikvah brings about a transformation from a state of Tumah (and all it implies) to a state of Teharah, clarity, openness, new life and vitality.

Chok / Unity, connecting to the "End Unto Itself"

It is firstly most important to understand that ultimately, the 'reason' immersion in a Mikvah purifies is beyond our comprehension. This is because, according to the Torah, immersion in a Mikvah is simply a *Chok* / a Mitzvah that transcends reason. Additionally, the laws of Tumah and Teharah are also in the category of Chok (*Tanchumah*, Chukas, 8). In the words of the Rambam, writing about the laws of Mikvah:

"It is a clear and apparent matter that the concepts of purity and impurity are Torah *decrees* (beyond rational reason) and they are not matters determined by a person's understanding; they are accordingly included in the category of Chukim (Chok). Similarly, immersion in a Mikvah to ascend from impurity is included in the category of Chukim, because impurity is not mud or filth that can be washed away with water" (Rambam, *Hilchos Mikvaos*, 11:12. *Sefer haChinuch*, Mitzvah 159).

Essentially, Mikvah is a supra-rational Mitzvah that exceeds the bounds of human logic. By contrast, a Mitzvah that is considered a *Mishpat* / ordinance, has a revealed 'ethical' rationale, such as, "Do not steal." However, from another perspective, all Mitzvos contain elements of Chok within their details. For example, while it is indeed ethical not to steal, the law for a thief who steals and simultaneously kills in the process is that he is liable for the death penalty, but he is not liable for what was stolen. This ruling is rooted in Torah and is quite simply 'beyond reason'.

On a deeper level, Chok is the very nature of each Mitzvah in its entirety.* The root of all Mitzvos must be be-

---

* Rabbi Chayim Brisker famously once said that we endeavor to understand 'what' the Torah or Gemara is telling us, not 'why'. This is because every Mitzvah is essentially a Chok, and we can therefore never understand the 'why' at its root. The *Ta'amim* / reasons provided for various Mishpatim are merely ideas and feelings of what these Mitzvos might mean to us (*Toras Chayim*, p. 82-83). This indeed is the Brisker *Derech Lamdus* / method of analytical learning. Parenthetically, we find

yond reason — reason alone cannot be the original cause of any Mitzvah, as it is Hashem who caused/commanded the Mitzvah, and that is ultimately why we adhere to it so faithfully. The world is preceded by Hashem's Torah and is created through Hashem's Torah, not the other way around. Having a real 'reason' for a Mitzvah would suggest that the world precedes the Torah, and that the world's needs stimulate particular responses from Above. But the Mitzvos actually exist prior to any worldly stimuli.

By definition, 'reason' suggests something extraneous to Unity. Reason means that there is a lack, something is 'missing' and it is being filled. Ultimately, as Mitzvos are rooted in the Essence and Absolute Simplicity of Hashem's Unity, there are no discernible reasons for Mitzvos. A Mitzvah is simply the unadulterated will of Hashem.

(in the Derech of Telz) that Rabbi Shimon Shkop probed the Mishpatim of the Torah to discover their Ta'am. He answers the question, why do our Sages say regarding money disputes המוציא מחבירו עליו הראיה / that if someone wants to extract money from someone else, they have to bring a clear proof that the money belongs to them, and thus ספק ממון לקולא / when in doubt concerning money the ruling is lenient, and the money stays with the person currently holding the money. Yet, there is also the principle that ספק אסור לחומרא / when in doubt concerning an *Isur* / prohibition from the Torah, the ruling is strict. So, why if a person argues that his money was stolen, a ספק אסור (as it is prohibited to steal), do we say לקולא and not extract the money from the one holding the money? Rabbi Shimon answers that in monetary issues we first must decide, logically, who can and does hold the money rightfully (thus המוציא מחבירו עליו הראיה is a *Sevara* / logical conclusion, *Baba Kama*, 46b), and only then do we apply the *Dinim* / laws of the Torah, *Sha'arei Yoshar*, Sha'ar 5, Chap. 1.

A Chok is, therefore, 'an end unto itself', rooted in the Oneness of Hashem which is the ultimate End unto Itself. And it is from that 'space' of Unity that all revelation, creation and illumination emerges. In this way, it is precisely the Chok aspect within the Mikvah that has the power to transform Tumah to Teharah. Tumah is rooted in and expresses a 'rational' scenario, as it were: 'It's all over, this is no longer vibrant, flowing, in process; I am stuck, hopeless, fixed, separate/alone.' People who are stuck in Tumah can find many reasons for their sense of *Yeiush* / giving up: 'I have trauma,' 'I could not get pregnant,' 'My loved one passed away,' 'I'm just set in my ways.' In order to move out of this space, they will eventually need to immerse themselves in the Source of Life above reason, that 'End unto Itself'; this is the supra-rational Chok quality of the Mikvah. To counter a sense of fixed finality or purposelessness, we need to immerse ourselves within a Mitzvah that is 'endless' and beyond purposes. From there can we emerge again, full of vitality, meaning, clarity and purpose.

And yet, just as the Essence of Hashem desired to reveal and manifest Divine Light in a way that could be appreciated in this world, the Mitzvos themselves tend to expand beyond the supra-rational category of Chok into the rational category of Mishpat. Therefore, "Although all the Chukim of the Torah are (supra-rational) 'decrees'…it is fit to meditate upon them, and wherever it is possible to provide a reason, one *should* provide a reason" (*Hilchos Temurah*, 4:13).

We, who are rooted in the Unity of Hashem, yet who function in a context of apparent duality, are created to seek meaning. We are programmed to think and function in a binary mode, making sense through reason and intuition, contrast and correspondence, physical form and mystical symbol, history and dreams of the future. Therefore, while keeping Unity in mind, we need also to explore the deeper reasons for the Mitzvah of Mikvah. We need to recognize that the laws of Tumah and Teharah, and thus Mikvah, are essentially Chukim, yet, "...wherever it is possible to provide reason, one should provide a reason." It will not be 'the' reason, rather 'a' reason, but we are meant to be fully engaged with the Mitzvos, including with our intellect; this is what Hashem wants from us — to exercise all of our finite capabilities to acknowledge and connect to the Infinite.

With the above understandings guiding us, let us begin to explore the literal, physical qualities of water and the subsequent sensations we experience when we come into contact with it.

The 'Reasons' for Mikvah: Water Brings Vitality & Freshness

Clearly, "Tumah is not mud or filth that can be washed away with water" (*Hilchos Mikvaos*, 11:12). Yet, there is a psycho-spiritual mechanism at work when we come in contact with water, certainly when we immerse in water. Even the act of washing one's hands with water can be therapeutic and healing.

A study showed that 'generally honest' people who lied, knowing that they lied and feeling bad about it, felt better about themselves if they washed their hands afterwards. There were two groups of people, placed in separate rooms, and each group was publically asked a question which the researchers knew most people would not answer truthfully. Both groups were then led out of their respected rooms through two separate corridors. One group passed a space with sinks and basins and were subliminally encouraged to wash their hands, and they did. The other group did not wash their hands. Later, when both groups assembled, they were asked questions about how they were feeling. Those who washed their hands were said to feel better about themselves than those who did not.

Even though washing one's hands does not get rid of negativity or a lie, yet, somehow, the mere act of pouring water, the visceral sensation of cool rivulets running off the hands, was subtly cathartic and inwardly/psychologically cleansing. How much more so is this true of a Mikvah, which gently welcomes the whole body into fresh, living waters. The more we are immersed in water, the more invigoration and renewal we experience.

Relatedly, our Sages tell us that although some people are

lenient and merely pour a certain amount of water over their bodies to expunge certain lesser forms of Tumah, those who are more diligent immerse completely into a Mikvah of 40 Sa'ah, "and Hashem lengthens their days and years" (Rashi on *Berachos*, 21a). "Longer" life means a fuller life, being fully alive every day, so that every day of your life is lengthened — this is what someone who immerses in a Mikvah receives. The 'reward' is completely in sync with the act itself. Immersing fully into a Mikvah of maximally alive, refreshing waters stimulates a maximally alive and fresh experience of life.

Water is arguably the only liquid that fully quenches our thirst and, additionally, leaves us feeling awake, alert and alive after we have immersed within it. Water is unique in other ways as well. "Water does not leave a *Roshem* / imprint on the body, in contrast (for example) to oil" (Rashash, *Nahar Shalom*, 40b. See also, *Radak* and *Rabbeinu Bachya* on Bereishis, 28:18). This does not mean that water does not have any effect on us, to the contrary, water is the embodiment of Chesed, the Divine quality of giving. It therefore imparts a powerful effect upon what or whomever it comes into contact with (*Eitz Chayim*, Sha'ar 39:13). However, the effect of water upon the person or object, in contrast to other fluids, is physically gentle. While certainly it has a powerful transformational effect upon a person who was Tamei, after a relatively short time, the body is completely dry again and one might not even notice that the body had been immersed in water at all. By contrast, if a person were to immerse in an oil, for example, it would be more invasive and leave a greater *Roshem* / imprint upon the body. In fact, it could take hours or even days to remove the Roshem of certain oils.

Water transforms us from one state to another, yet leaves us feeling free and unencumbered, without imposing any residue of heaviness.

Lightly-Cooled Mikvah

The above is one visceral reason to immerse specifically in a Mikvah in which the temperature mimics the body's temperature, rather than being steaming hot. Hot water relaxes the body but also tends to induce lethargy and heaviness.

Cooler water, on the other hand, awakens, refreshes and activates. To shed the psycho-spiritual lethargy and heaviness of Tumah, and to be catapulted into the aliveness and openness of Teharah, cooler water is more experientially effective, although halachically there is no difference between cold and hot water.

It is for this reason, perhaps, that some sources speak of specifically immersing in a cooler, or at least not very hot, Mikvah (*Teharos haKodesh*, Mikvah Yisrael, 5). "Like *Mayim Karim* / cold waters to a weary soul", says the verse in Mishlei / Proverbs (25:25). קרים / *Karim* is the same letters as קרי /

Keri / released seed, plus a Mem which stands for *Mikvah* (*Sur meRa' veAsei Tov*, Sur meRa', Shevi'is). Colder water wakes us up, animates us and stimulates an existential, mental and emotional vitality.

Mayim Karim in its numeric value is 440, which is the same as the word *Mes* / dead (*Magid Talumah* [Dinov], Berachos, 22a. *Sur meRa' v'Asei Tov*, ibid). This *Gematria* / numerical equivalence informs us that to remove the 'deadness' of Tumah and return one to a sense of tangible vitality, it can help to immerse in a Mayim Karim Mikvah.

As mentioned, water is associated with Chesed (*Zohar* 2, 159b), giving and sustaining life. Heat is often associated with the quality of Gevurah, severity, constriction and rigidity; this could be another reason to immerse in a Mikvah that is not unnaturally hot, as we are seeking to reinvigorate ourselves.

If colder water is a little uncomfortable for you, or if you are immersing in a natural spring and the waters may be very cold, try to embrace and include this discomfort within your intentions during immersion. Rabbi Eliyahu de Vidas (1518-1592), the author of *Reishis Chochmah*, writes that we know that a Mikvah is like *Olam haBa* / a glimmer of the World to Come. We also know that "Three precious gifts were given to us, all of which were given by means of *Yesurim* / hardship and difficulties: the Torah, the Land of Israel and Olam haBa" (*Berachos*, 5a). And so, if you have

Yesurim from the cold, think about how you are opening/ preparing yourself to receive the gift of Olam haBa through your discomfort (*Reishis Chochmah*, Sha'ar haAhavah, 11). Also, do not worry about catching a cold, as he also writes, no harm will come to a person who immerses in a Mikvah, as one is entering into the Name of Hashem (*Ibid*), which will protect them from any adverse effects. We also know that the Baal Shem Tov personally guaranteed that he would take responsibility for the effects of one's immersion, and it will thus not cause them any harm (*Mishmeres Shalom*, 2).

This is not to suggest that the waters should be ice-cold, just not boiling hot. A Mikvah slightly below body temperature can be optimal to magnify the subsequent psycho-physical refreshment and aliveness that one experiences as a result of their immersion. It should be pointed out that the Alter Rebbe, Rabbi Schneur Zalman, fought strongly despite opposition, to heat Mikvaos for women, certainly in the cold climate of Russia.* But, of course, in that time and place, an

---

* It appears from the Gemara that we should not heat a Mikvah (*Berachos*, 22a). "Is there such a thing as immersion in hot water? Hot water is drawn water" (*Ta'anis*, 13a). Rabbeinu Tam and the Ri' write that heated Mikvaos are not Kosher, because people will confuse a Mikvah for a bathhouse (see also *Mordechai*, Shavuos, Hilchos Mikvaos, Siman 703. The Beis Yoseph brings down the Mordechai, *Yoreh De'ah*, end of Siman 201, and rules as such in his Shulchan Aruch). The Beis Yoseph, who lived mostly in warmer climates (later in life in Israel), writes that there are those who forbid throwing a hot iron, for example, into a Mikvah to heat up the water (*Yoreh De'ah*, 201:74). The Rama, who lived in colder climates (Eastern Europe) writes (*Ibid*) that there are those who are lenient, although in a place where there is no custom, we should be

unheated Mikvah was literally a freezing cold one. Many women performed *Mesiras Nefesh* / self-sacrifice, and immersed even when they had to literally crack the ice covering the waters. But some were not able to build up the courage to do this, and as a result they were not intimate with their spouses, and so the Alter Rebbe championed the heated Mikvah.

It is important to note that while a highly heated men's Mikvah is certainly Kosher, cooler waters have a more enlivening effect on the person immersing. Nevertheless, there are also times when hot water is better and perhaps even required. For instance, hot water is certainly required for *Rechitzah* / washing oneself on Erev Shabbos, before immersing in a Mikvah (*Shulchan Aruch*, Orach Chayim, Siman

---

more strict (*Aruch haShulchan*, Yoreh De'ah, 201:216). There are also sources that write that the Beis Yoseph, at the end of his life, was more lenient regarding heated Mikvoas (*Shu't, Nivchar M'Kesef*, Siman 17), and today even Sefardic Jews heat their Mikvaos.

In previous times, most Mikvaos were cold, but in very cold climates, such as in White Russia where the Alter Rebbe lived, cold water could be dangerous in the winter. Also, since the water was very cold many hurried their immersion and did not immerse properly. The Alter Rebbe thus argued that Mikvaos could be heated, and he approved a system for doing so. Many contended against him for Halachic reasons (as above), but in the end, virtually everyone today heats their Mikvaos one way or another. The Alter Rebbe's system is explained and defended by his grandson, the Tzemach Tzedek (*Teshuvos Tzemach Tzedek*, Yoreh De'ah, 176:3:2 and 334), for the above two reasons. The *Aruch haShulchan*, who also lived in cold climates, and studied and visited the Tzemach Tzedek, ruled the same.

260:1), and in this case, according to most rulings, not even lukewarm water will suffice (*Noda beYehudah*, 2:24). Scrubbing with hot water helps release accumulated dirt, sweat, stagnant oils and dead skin cells. The heat also causes a release of tension, helping us to let go of the past week, so that we can enter a Shabbos mood with peace and relaxation. Yet, after the hot shower or bath, it is still beneficial to enter a cooler Mikvah and feel the invigoration. Again, the Mikvah itself is not about cleansing and Teharah is not about hygiene, but rather about becoming more alive.

Transforming, Becoming — the Nature of Water

All spiritual growth and movement is stimulated by Chesed, just as water, the physical manifestation of Chesed, stimulates the growth of vegetation (*Eitz Chayim*, Sha'ar haYerach, Sha'ar 35. *Likutei Levi Yitzchak*, He'aros leZohar, Bereishis, 92). Water is also characterized by *Tenuah* / movement*, as explored previously;

---

* Fire is also defined by Tenuah, movement, as is wind. In fact, the the the nature of the Three Primary Elements (fire, wind and water) is movement, whereas the inner/secondary element of earth that is within everything, is stationary (*Netzach Yisrael*, 57). Since the nature of a flame is movement, it jumps upward (*Tanya*, Chap 19. Rambam, *Hilchos Yesodei haTorah*, 4:2), and is thus related to a Mikvah of transformation. Indeed, "The main form of immersion should be in fire" (*Sanhedrin*, 39a), however this not a real possibility (see *Maharsha* ad loc). The *Shach*, (Shemos, 20:1), writes that the people of Israel, at Sinai, immersed in the "River Dinor" before receiving the Torah. The River of Dinor (*Daniel*, 7:10) is a "river of fire" (*Zohar* 2, 254a. See also, *Chagigah*, 12b). Yet, in actuality, according to Halacha, *Ein Lach Tumah She'eino Olah Elah Al*

it therefore has the power to inspire, arouse and propel us into a state of greater openness and dynamic fluidity.

Water, which is constantly moving, is thus the elemental agent of transition and transformation. If everything in the world was static and solid, like the element of earth, nothing would ever change. Due to the *Chesed* / kindness of water, people and things that are immersed within it can soften and flow into a new form or pattern.

It is important to note, however, that Tenuah can also be purely cyclical, and without any real progress or growth. In other words, something can 'move' from a today to a tomorrow, but if the movement is confined to a cyclical, fixed and predictable pattern, without any connection to the Infinite, there is no real chance for development or evolution; this kind of circular motion is thus nothing more than a movement that always returns to square one. It is a fixed, closed system, with no possibility of redemption.

Water, besides being motile and fluid, is also without a fixed Tzurah, definition or identity, as discussed. Therefore it is always in a state of becoming, adapting, transforming and looking to the future. Water is never satisfied with what is, but is constantly reaching and striving for what could be.

Yedei Aish / there is no Tumah that is dispelled by fire alone" Rambam, *Hilchos Ma'achalos Assuros*, 17:5.

These two aspects, constant movement and inherent form-lessness, are what allow for the qualities of progressive movement and perpetual change.

Questioning What Is, becoming What Could Be

The element of water is intimately connected to the questioning concept of *Mah* / What? (*Toldos Yaakov Yoseph. Degel Machanei Ephrayim*, Vaera. Incidentally, the word *Mayim* is numerically 90, twice *Mah* / 45). To live in a state of Mah means to be open to the unknown, free from fixed definitions. This allows one to always be available to growth and learning. To approach life from a state of Mah is to live constantly connected to the 'endless waters' of possibility, and the deep joy of becoming.

In addition to its *Mah* nature, the word *Mayim* contains the word *Mi* / Who. (Incidentally, *Yam* / ocean is *Mi* backwards.) The Zohar, in its *Hakdamah* / introduction, speaks of two types of questions: *Mah* and *Mi*. 'What?' is a lower form of question, according to the Zohar. Similarly, Rashi writes that "What is this?" (*Shemos*, 13:14) is a question of the Simple Child, as in the Pesach Haggadah, who does not know how to pose a detailed question, and asks only in the most general terms. 'What?' is an unsophisticated desire for an external, factual definition. 'Who,' on the other hand, is a higher level inquiry, expressing a desire to know the identity or source of phenomena, and its relationship with oneself and others. *Mi* alludes to a more existential and relational level of contemplation: Who am I and to Whom am I relating?

When we immerse ourselves in a Mikvah, we are entering into an open place of both *Mah* / what and *Mi* / who. The words *Tibul* / 'immersed' and *Bitul* / 'nullification' or 'transparency' contain the same letters. This means that when we are Tibul, we are experiencing a Bitul of our old 'what' and our old 'who'; we are thus able to shed our old, fixed definition, as well as our old, limited identity. When we let go of these, new awareness and states of being can emerge. Empowerment and aliveness burst forth with the birth of this new, holy self that we are in the process of becoming.

Like all other living mammals, we need oxygen to breathe and live. We need to inhale and exhale continuously in order to exist. Thus, by submerging our entire body in water, we 'cease to exist', as it were. Once a person has ceased breathing, he is considered dead (*Yumah*, 85a. Rambam *Hilchos Shabbos,* 2:19; *Shulchan Aruch,* Orach Chayim 329:4). In this way, when we are fully immersed in water, we temporarily cease to be among the living. There is a nullification of self as if we have 'died' for a moment. There is an absence of the 'what' and even of the 'who' of self, a letting go which allows us to receive a new "breath of life" when we emerge from the waters.

In the same way, we are also able to let go of all our problems, issues and struggles, as well as all of our cravings and attachments to the fixed world of death, separation and negativity. We enter the space of *Ayin* / no-thing-ness, so that a higher, *Yesh Tahor* / pure existence can arise from the Mikvah.

For any Yesh to transform or morph into any other Yesh there needs to be a return to Ayin in between. For example, if you want to make a table into a chair, you first need to deconstruct the table, and then you can construct a chair. This deconstruction is the aspect and experience of Ayin. Water, from a mammal's perspective, is Ayin. Because we cannot breathe under water, our Yesh is not tolerated or supported in this element. Therefore, in order to become a free people, Klal Yisrael as a whole needed to traverse the sea. In other words, they needed to pass through water and let go of their old Yesh (slave existence), before they could be birthed into their new Yesh as a free people. Their passage through the sea was thus like passing through a birth canal. It was the Ayin between the old and the new Yesh. Similarly, immersing in a Mikvah is entering into the place of Ayin, as we are ceasing to breathe and thus ceasing to be, as it were, so that we can become a new existence.

When we are underwater, we are no longer inhabiting or inhibited by our past status. Interestingly, in this moment we have shed our old Yesh, but we are not yet our new selves. According to Halacha, it is only when a person *emerges* from the Mikvah that he or she is actually purified; until a person leaves the Mikvah, they are not yet Tahor (*Kesef Mishnah*, on the Rambam *Hilchos Avos haTumah*, 6:16. Perhaps an earlier source is *Tosefos*, Shabbos, 35a, "veYarad". See however, *Pri Yitzchak*, 2, Siman 35. *Avnei Neizer*. Choshen Mishpat, Siman 72. *Devar Avraham*, Hashmatos, 2:15). Perhaps it could also be said that a person is no longer Tamei once immersed within the water, as they are no longer the old Yesh; however, they are not yet considered Tahor. They are in between states. It is only when exiting the water that one truly becomes a new Yesh. The new you, Tahor and transparent, is fully assumed only once you leave the Ayin of the water, and emerge again onto the dry land of Yesh.

As demonstrated above, water is a manifestation of the *Ma'amar Echad* / the First Utterance of Creation. With the Ma'amar Echad, all of existence (all Yesh) was created in a unified potential. Water is the *Ayin* / pure potential that precedes and includes all subsequent *Yeshus* / something-ness.

To be clear, there are two levels of Ayin. There is a state of Ayin that transcends all 'somethings', and there is a deeper state of Ayin that includes all 'somethings' in potential. The Ayin of the Ma'amar Echad is the potential of all things, all particularities and all life.

When you immerse fully within the Ayin, the Ma'amar Echad of the Mikvah, you are not only letting go of the old, but also unifying with the infinite potential of the person that you can become. But to actually emerge as that new person, you need to emerge from the water.

A Body of Water Shaped as a Square: A Closed Womb

As explained, water is without *Tzurah* / shape (*Gevuros Hashem*, 23); without any external imposition or definition/boundaries, it is formless. Yet, when it is placed within a vessel, it effortlessly takes shape and form. Water in a glass assumes the posture/contours of the glass. The waters of the Mikvah are in themselves formless, however the walls of the Mikvah give the water a particular shape.

You may have noticed that most man-made Mikvaos (as opposed to natural bodies of water such as the ocean or a pooled spring) are square or exhibit a square-like shape. They are rarely round or oval. This is intentional.

Many sources suggest that a constructed Mikvah should be like the square shape of a closed final Mem (*Tikkunei Zohar*, Tikkun 19). Besides the shape of the final Mem, a square has four sides, which correspond to the four letters in the Name of Hashem, the Yud-Hei-Vav-Hei, as will be further explored.*

_____

* Another reason for the cubical shape: there are 9 'points' on each side of

Sefer Yetzirah (3:4) speaks of three Mother Letters: Aleph, which corresponds to *Avir* / wind, Mem, connected to *Mayim* / water, and Shin, which is related to *Aish* / fire. Thus, Mem stands for *Mayim* (*Sefer haBahir*, 85). *Mikvah* also begins with the letter Mem. Numerically, the letter Mem is 40, alluding to the 40 Sa'ah of water that define the minimum requirement for a Kosher Mikvah. In the Torah, 40 is the number of transformation: 40 days of the *Mabul* / flood which submerged and purified the world, and 40 years in the Desert, in which an enslaved people was transformed into a free people.

Even deeper, the 40 days of rain that brought about the Great Mabul correspond to the 40 days of *Yetziras haVelad* / the formation of the Tzurah of a child (*Rashi*, Bereishis, 7:4. *Medrash Rabbah*, Bereishis, 32:5). In other words, there are 40 days from the moment of conception until the point when we can say that the fetus has the form of a 'child' (*Nidah*, 30a. *Kerisus*, 10a. See also: *Berachos*, 60a. *Sotah*, 2a).

Indeed, before these 40 days have elapsed, the fetus is considered like 'water', called *Mayim b'Alma* / mere water (*Yevamos*, 69b), because the child has no Tzurah yet. The child is

---

the Mikvah: each line or edge of the cube has three points, beginning, middle and end, plus a point in the center of the edge. Adding all of these points together produces a sum of 40 points, corresponding to the 40 Sa'ah of the Mikvah. See also: *Reishis Chochmah*, Sha'ar haAhavah, 11. Shaloh, *Sha'ar haOsyos*, Kedushah, 13. *Teshuvos Maharsham* 4-5, Siman 114. *Bnei Yissachar*, Elul, Ma'amar 1:15. Tzemach Tzedek, *Sefer haLikutim*, Mikvah, p. 1,458.

not yet definable as female or male. During these first 40 days, we can still pray that the baby become a particular gender, and this is not considered a "wasted prayer" (*Berachos*, 60a). This is because, like water, the child is still in the state of un-shaped potential.

From one perspective, every fetus begins life as 'female'. Only later do the hormones that form the traits of a male body begin to create a differentiated gender. Accordingly, all children actually begin life as females and then later the 'potential' males branch out into masculinity. In this sense, the feminine is the foundational essence of life, the *Chomer* / pure substance of identity, and the masculine is the *Tzurah* / the articulated, manifest form (Maharal). In either case, both genders ultimately begin life as raw existence, as 'water', with no fixed Tzurah or Yesh, and only after 40 days does a particular form emerge. Before that, the child is 'water within water', and thus in a state of pure potential.

Furthermore, for the entire duration of the growth of the fetus, we are immersed in an amniotic sac, a bag of clear liquid that helps to cushion the baby and provide it with the fluids that allow it to 'breathe' and swallow. We exist in water and as water. Our immersion in water lasts throughout the pregnancy, as we develop and grow within the womb. When the amniotic sac breaks, usually at the beginning of the birth process, it is thus fittingly called the 'breaking of the water'.

When we enter into a Mikvah, we are returning back to the pure embryonic state prior to any defined form. We return to the place of being 'mere water', prior to gender and a defined identity, free from all negativity, transgression, Tumah and connection to the fixity and finality of 'death'.

Entering into the 40 Sa'ah, the Mem of the Mikvah, is to go back into the Ayin, the pure Chomer (prima materia), to the place of our pure potential. Immersion returns us to the Ma'amar Echad before the differentiation of Creation. We enter into the space where the *Yetziras haVelad* / formation of the 'child' (the individual) is taking place. We consciously return to the womb, the 'Mem' of Creation, so that we can undo any negativity that we have created or accumulated, and emerge as a new, unburdened creature.

A question remains: why should a Mikvah be constructed specifically in the shape of a *closed* Mem, a 'final Mem'? If a regular Mem is appropriate for the words *Mikvah* and *Mayim*, and to symbolize transformation through its numeric value of 40, why not construct the Mikvah in the shape of a regular Mem?

A closed Mem represents the feminine (Arizal, *Likutei Torah*, Lech Lecha), and is similar to a closed womb that completely envelops the fetus (*Sha'ar haPesukim*, Tehilim, 18. See also regarding the 'male womb' *Sefer haBahir*, 84). Spiritually, the closure is for holding in and absorbing the inner light, in preparation to release, give birth and become a *Mashpia* / giver (*Mashpia* also starts with the letter Mem). When this closed womb of potential finally gives birth, it becomes an 'open Mem' (*Sefer haBahir*, 85). An open Mem suggests that it is in the state of actually being Mashpia (*Pardes Rimonim*, Sha'ar haOsyos, Mem. Tzemach Tzedek, *Sefer haLikutim*, Mikvah, p. 1,458). But until then, the womb must be a completely sealed enclosure to protect and nurture the process of becoming that is occurring within it.

Therefore, when we immerse ourselves in a Mikvah, we are entering into the supernal, closed Womb of Creation, which contains the potential of all possible birth. We are like "a fetus hidden within her mother's womb" (*Reishis Chochmah*, Sha'ar haAhavah, 11). Through immersion, we are returning to the primordial state of Creation, in preparation to being 'reborn' (*Sefer haChinuch*, Mitzvah 173). As we immerse, we enclose ourselves and nullify ourselves within the womb of Ayin. We close the door on all of our stagnancy, anxiety and depression, in order to become a pure embryo. Then, finally, we open the womb to birth ourselves as a freshly-formed conscious being.

This is why we immerse in a 'closed' shape, like a final letter Mem. Still, the question remains: there are other closed shapes, so why do we immerse in the specific image of a square or cube? Everything is by Divine orchestration; the fact that the final Mem is a square and not a round or oval shape, and that we immerse in a pool that is shaped like a square or rectangle, suggests something profound.

A circle or oval shape represents Infinity, with no beginning or end, whereas a square or rectangle represents definition, limitation and finitude. A circle represents wheel-like movement, whereas a square represents something stable or stationary (*Medrash Pinchas*, Shabbos). The Mikvah is box-shaped because the *Tachlis* / ultimate purpose is not only that we move out of our old 'boxes' into a world of ceaselessly circular infinity, but to emerge from the Mikvah in a new, stable structure in order to stand firmly on dry land again. Our goal is not to remain submerged in water, so to speak, to live as nullified, formless beings forever. The goal of the Mikvah is to bring a refreshing *Reshimu* / residue of the Infinite, the Ayin, the circle-world, down into the 'square' world of definitions, stability and Yesh of our daily life in the world. We are meant to actively build up this world, not just passively roll through it, or be rolled over by it.

Rabban Shimon ben Gamliel says, "There is nothing naturally square in Creation" (Yerushalmi, End of *Ma'asros*. *Nedarim*, 3:2. *Shavuos* 3:8. Whether this is the opinion of all Sages, and whether 'square' means a perfect square, and whether this only refers to human beings, and so forth, are questions that are greatly debated. The Rebbe, *Igros Kodesh*, Vol. 2, 360). However, this means that from the *Infinite Creator's* perspective nothing is a finite box; everything is Ayin and endless infinity. From this Divine perspective, Hashem is the *Yesh haAmiti* / True Existence, while Creation is no-thing-ness, devoid of all 'things' and thus borderless and infinite.

Yet, from our perspective, the finite world is the 'true', tangible existence; everything in this world is bordered or 'square', as it were. In fact, the first *Tzimtzum* / concealment of the Infinite Light, is called the 'Tzimtzum of the Square', since from our perspective, after the concealment of the circle of Infinity, bounded 'squareness' came into existence. While the revealed, finite world of Yesh is square, everything beyond this world is *Ayin* / Infinite Transcendence and circle-reality.

In our human paradigm of squareness, we need to construct 'boxes' that have the capacity to reveal the Infinite Light of the Creator within our reality. Hashem wants us to live in the manifest 'boxed' world and reveal Hashem's Presence within these boxes, which represent the finite metrics of the world. But the challenge in accomplishing this is to not get stuck, limited and entirely defined by our boxes. We need to find and draw down transcendence, flow and Teharah within the boxes of our life, within the Tzurah of the world. This is also the reason why the shapes of the *Beis haMik-dash* / Holy Temple, the *Aron* / holy Ark, and the *Luchos* / tablets, were all box-like. Their objective was to facilitate the marriage of Heaven and earth, the Infinite potential with the finite Tzurah. "And they shall make Me a sanctuary

(Mishkan and Beis haMikdash, *Eiruvin* 2a) and I will dwell בתוכם / in their midst" (*Shemos*, 25:8). The word בתוכם can also mean בתוך / within the ם (*Megaleh Amukos*, Terumah, 5). The objective of the Beis haMikdash is to draw down and make a dwelling place for Hashem's presence within the square Mem of dimensional reality.

Rainwater & Box Shaped Mikvah

This dynamic of formlessness within form is not only reflected in the 'vessel' of the Mikvah itself, meaning, the shape and walls of the Mikvah, but also in the nature of the water within the Mikvah. Most human-built Mikvaos contain rainwater, which is vividly formless, falling freely from out of the unbounded sky. And yet, on a deeper level, rainwater exhibits this dynamic of formlessness within form as well; the non-Tzurah within a larger Tzurah.

To explain: on a physical level, the most basic type of rain consists of liquid water in the form of airborne droplets which become heavy enough to fall from the sky under the pull of gravity. The droplets themselves come from condensed atmospheric water vapor that collects and rises. As the *Pasuk* / verse says, "And a mist ascended from the earth and (thus) watered the entire surface of the ground" (*Bereishis*, 2:6). The atmospheric water vapor ascends, condenses and then descends as rain to water the surface of the ground.

On a deeper level, *Chazal* / our Sages argue regarding the metaphysical root of rain (*Ta'anis*, 9b). Rabbi Eliezer says the whole world draws its water supply from the waters of the earth's oceans, as literally implied by the verse: "And a mist ascended from the earth and watered the entire surface of the ground." Rabbi Yehoshua said, the whole world drinks from the Upper Waters, as implied by another verse: "From the Rain of Heaven you shall have water" (*Devarim*, 11:11). In a similar fashion, the Medrash (*Bereishis Rabbah*) records that Rabbi Yochanan is of the opinion that rain comes from Heavenly 'upper clouds', whereas Reish Lakish argues that rain comes from 'lower clouds'.

These are the two basic opinions, the rains originate either from above or below, but there is a third teaching recorded in the Medrash *Pirkei d'Rebbe Eliezer*. This teaching says, "When we perform the will of Hashem, we receive water from Above; and when we do not, we receive water from the Lower Waters." It could be said that this Medrash is essentially a reconciliation between the two opposing opinions. In other words, the source of rain is not an actual argument between R. Eliezer and R. Yehoshua or R. Yochanan and Reish Lakish, rather, both positions are correct; the source of rain changes depending on the level of consciousness and behavior of the People of Israel.

"When we perform the will of Hashem we receive water from Above" — this is because our *Avodah* / work in this world is to 'connect' Heaven and earth and when we are doing so, we receive water from Heaven (*Aderes Eliyahu*, Bereishis, 2:6). There is an objective correlation between the way we live and the way Hashem responds to us. And when we are aligned with the One Above, we are able to receive nourishment that emanates directly from the One Above.

Physically, rain always originates from the same place, but the meta-root of life-giving waters changes with our mindset and behavior. When we are doing the Avodah of bringing Heaven down to Earth, connecting the spiritual with the physical, our rain similarly manifests from Heaven to below; our sustenance and nourishment comes directly from the One Above in a way that is palpable and perceivable.

"The day of *Geshamim* / 'the rains' is as great as the day on which *Shamayim v'haAretz* / 'the Heavens and the earth' were created" (*Ta'anis*, 7b). The role of rain in relation to the creation of Heaven and earth is that rain *unifies* Heaven and earth, like the *v'* / letter Vav in *Shamayim-v'haAretz*.

Shamayim / Heaven is without *Tzurah* / form. The word *Shamayim* alludes to *Sham Mayim* / 'water is there' (*Chagigah*, 12a). In other words, the main element of Heaven is 'water' or formless *Chomer* / potentiality. When rainwater flows down and irrigates the element of *Afar* / earth, formlessness penetrates the defined *Tzurah* / form of earth, and marries the reality of pure, Infinite spirituality with the physical world. In fact, the most common Hebrew word for rain / *Geshem* is etymologically related to the word *Gashmiyus* / physicality. (*Rabbeinu Bachya,* Devarim, 11:17), further highlighting its function of unifying the formless potential with finite form. Geshem is quite literally the way the *Shefa* / flow from Above, pure potential, becomes manifest in the Tzurah of Gashmiyus.

In summary: the element of water is without Tzurah, representing infinite potential, while the element of earth has the quality of defined Tzurah, permanence, solidity and stability. A world with only 'water', with only pure, raw, formless potential, would be constantly changing and nothing would be permanent or consistent. On the other hand, a world with only the element of earth and no water would resist all movement and change. There must be some degree of continuity and definition for life to manifest and function, and yet there must also be room to grow and develop. We therefore need both Ayin and Yesh in a balanced coexistence. Rain metaphorically (and literally) brings about this coexistence. It allows the Ayin above to become manifest within the Yesh below. This is one deeper reason why rainwater specifically is used for square-shaped Mikvaos.

CHAPTER 5

~~~

Land Creatures
Submerged in Water

ACCORDING TO THE TORAH, TO CLEANSE OUR-SELVES OF RITUAL IMPURITY WE NEED TO IMMERSE OUR ENTIRE BODY IN WATER. Even if a single strand of hair remains above the water, the person does not transition from a state of ritual impurity to ritual purity.

Our life and our habitat is on dry land; this is where we breathe, build and flourish. Under water, with no oxygen, we cease to breathe, and for that brief moment, we cease to be. This is necessary for our process of transformation. In order for us to shed our old misaligned *Tzurah* / form and existence, we need to expose ourselves completely, but brief-ly, to the formlessness of non-being. There, in the absence of Tzurah, a new form can be gestated and reconfigured: a healthy Tzurah that can be a strong and flexible vessel for bringing Heaven down to earth and unifying them.

When we *Tovel* / immerse, not only we are *Batel* / egoless, but we open ourselves to experience a state of *Achdus* / uni-ty consciousness. There are 960 *Lugin* / measures of water in a Mikvah, and the words *Shema Yisrael* equal 960 (*Maor vaShemesh*, Hashmatos, Vayera). To truly declare *Shema Yisrael... Hashem Echad* / "Listen O Israel, Hashem is an Absolute Unity" we need to be in a posture of total Bitul and self-sac-rifice; we need to offer up our stubborn, dualistic ego and let it temporarily be put to rest. In fact, there are sources that suggest staying underwater until you can hardly bear holding your breath any longer (*Sefer haMidos*, Hamtakas haDin, 54). This is a more dramatic expression and visceral experience of 'ceasing to be' when immersed in the Mikvah. This is the necessary formlessness that one must enter into as they leave their old form behind and emerge in a whole new Tzurah. It is, of course, vitally important to avoid putting yourself into any risk of physical danger when engaging in such a practice.

Mentally Divesting from Materiality

Because of the vivid experience of *Bitul* / non-being that it gives us access to, Mikvah is arguably the practice most conducive to achieving the sought after spiritual state of *Hispashtus haGashmiyus* / divestment of all sense of materiality. Experiencing some form of Hispashtus is integral for *Tefilah* / prayer specifically, and essential for a person's *Avodah* / spiritual work and attainment of deeper spiritual awareness in general. In addition to the importance of Mikvah before Tefilah, immersion in a Mikvah is indispensable to truly comprehend and contemplate the Sod, the deeper mysteries of the Torah. The Baal Shem Tov once said that all the spiritual levels he attained were due to frequent immersions in the Mikvah (*Likutei Yekarim*, Yosher Divrei Emes, 42. *Notzer Chesed*, 6:8). Anything that demands a *Hecherkeit* / a sense of elevation, or of being connected to something that is higher and deeper than oneself and their immediate surroundings, demands immersion in the Mikvah (see at length, *Sefer HaSheim*, by the Rokeach, in the beginning).

Regarding Tefilah, our Sages tell us that the *Chasidim haRishonim* / Early Pious Ones would *Sho'im* / tarry one hour before their Tefilah and for one hour after their Tefilah (*Berachos*, 32b). Literally, *Sho'im* means to 'wait', but it specifically implies an act of becoming still. They would settle their minds and quiet their thoughts, becoming completely still, and only then commence prayer from that place of inner focus. The 'waiting' was intended to clear their consciousness of all distractions in preparation for fully-engaged prayer (Rambam, *Pirush haMishnayos*, Berachos 5:1).

The word *Sho'im* can also be turned more deeply inward: not simply to clear the mind, but to clear themselves of any sense of being a separate, ego-self. The Early Chasidim would actually empty themselves of all ego (R. Mendel of Vitepsk, *Pri Ha'aretz*, Vayakhel-Pekudei. Magid of Koznitz. *Avodas Yisroel*, p. 164), and they would attain a degree of Hispashtus haGashmiyus. They would internally isolate and detach themselves from the material nature of their body and physical sensations.

Although full Hispashtus haGashmiyus involves a high level of spiritual development, the *Shulchan Aruch* rules that it is something every person should aspire to achieve — on their level — prior to commencing Tefilah (*Tur*, Orach Chayim, 98. See also Shaloh, *Asara Hilulim*, p. 319. *Nefesh haChayim*, Sha'ar

2:14). Indeed, when a person prays from this non-attached state, their prayers are 'selfless' and, in turn, redemptive — not just for themselves, but for the entire world.

Parenthetically, engaging this practice of 'divestment of materiality' does not necessarily mean that the practitioner forgets about their body or its needs. However, the practitioner does begin to function in a state of detachment from the inherent selfishness of physicality, and is then able, after prayer, to reintegrate into the world of physicality in a rectified and unified way.

Going to the Mikvah is a fitting time to achieve, at least mentally, a degree of Hispashtus; this is one way to follow the ruling of the *Shulchan Aruch* and connect to the practice of the Early Chasidim. Not only does being underwater involve a shedding of the material, physical sense of the body, the entire process of going into the Mikvah is an exercise of Hispashtus, as explored. For instance, taking off your garments before immersing is literally a kind of Hispashtus, divestment or disrobing. By slowly undressing, garment by garment, there is a visceral sensation of letting go a sense of peeling away the layers of your being and garments of your identity.

Hispashtus Meditation Before Immersion

Prior to entering the Mikvah, when you are about to remove your garments, notice what you are wearing. Feel the weight of your clothing and the quality of the fabric on your body. Imagine each piece of clothing as an extraneous layer, concealing or inhibiting your inner aliveness and the authentic expression of who you are. Let these outer garments symbolize the constrictive *Levushim* / inner garments of your soul, your Tamei thoughts, words and actions. When you are taking off these garments you are also removing the weight that presses down on your heart, the stress that chafes your skin, and the fog that clouds the vision of your inner eyes.

Allow each piece of clothing to drop, one after the other, feeling the pressure of your past actions, words and thoughts falling away. Continue in this manner until you are completely unclothed, free of all baggage, light and relieved.

Now that you have gone through a Hispashtus of garments, as you slowly descend the steps into the Mikvah, notice how the water is receiving you unquestioningly. With each step, you are more enveloped and embraced. Not only have you dropped your external garments of thoughts, words and actions, but now, under the water, you can let go of your body itself. You can 'take off' your very identity as a limited being, returning to the womb-like state of 'water within water'.

A physical action has the power to initiate an inner response, stimulating a shift in consciousness and mindset.

In the words of the Chinuch, "The heart (consciousness) is drawn after the actions" (*Sefer haChinuch*, Mitzvah 16). For example, cleaning your room makes you feel more organized and psychologically 'put together'. Donning elegant, clean clothes puts you in touch with the royal glory of Shabbos. Likewise, the physical acts of removing garments and submerging in water can stimulate a shift in consciousness. They can inspire a letting go of negative thoughts and actions, and even a brief transcendence of the body and its needs. The act of physical Hispashtus propels you toward a mental, emotional and spiritual Hispashtus.

Letting Go to Be Rebirthed

The purpose of *Hispashtus haGashmiyus* / releasing the body is not to completely abandon one's body, but rather to become more consciously embodied. Indeed, the ultimate Divine purpose of our lives on earth is for us to be engaged with the body and the physical world in such a way that Hashem's Infinite Presence may rest and reveal Itself within this finite realm of existence. It is not enough just to let go, although this is an essential first step. We are not trying to live forever under the timeless waters of the Mikvah; the ultimate purpose of the Mikvah only manifests when we exit the Mikvah and emerge as a rebirthed self. It is then that we are able to redress ourselves within rectified garments of thought, speech and action, by bringing the residue of self-nullification we experienced in the waters of

Mikvah into the 'square' or limited world of space, time and relationships.

Simply put, we return to the Divine womb in order to be reborn and recreated. In the language of our Sages, a person or object immersed in a Mikvah is called *Zeria* / planting. When we immerse in the Mikvah, we are like a seed being implanted within the earth, nullified within the ground, and sprouting forth as a new tree (see *Rashi*, Beitza, 17b).

The first letters of the words ברא טהור לב / "Create (in me) a pure heart (O G-d)" (Tehilim, 51:12) can be rearranged to form the word טבל / *Tovel* / to immerse, and the last letters are an acronym for the word ברא / *Bara* / create. This teaches us that someone who is 'Tovel' in a Mikvah is 'created' anew; they are a *Beriyah Chadashah* / a new creation (Arizal, *Sha'ar Halikutim*, Tehilim, 51. Shaloh, *Sha'ar haOsyos*, Teharah, 11. The Baal Shem Tov teaches that *Mikvah* is related to the Divine Name *Ei-led* / giving birth, as will be later explored).

This transformative power of the Mikvah is encoded into the number 40. As discussed previously, there are 40 Sa'ah of water in a Mikvah, which are equal to 960 Lugin. Similarly, in 40 days there are 960 hours ($24 \times 40 = 960$). Moshe was on the mountain for 40 days, or 960 hours (*Megaleh Amukos*, 153, 247. *Regel Yishara* [Dinov], Ma'areches Mem, Mikvah). This is also the same *time* period in which an embryo is transformed into a fetus. The number 40 is thus a symbol of transformation. A Mikvah is a representation of this pattern within *space*. When we enter the gestational space of the Mikvah, we can become a new person.

In the words of the Chinuch, "The reason for [immersing in] water...is that a person, after immersing, should imagine himself, *as if he was just born*, this very moment, just as when the world was covered with water, before the creation of man.... He should take to heart and use the power of his imagination, that just as he is experiencing renewal on a bodily level, he will likewise be [spiritually] renewed and [inspired to] perform good deeds" (*Sefer haChinuch*, Mitzvah 173).

Water Helps in Giving Birth

Giving birth demands making space for a new entity, and this means one needs to be flexible and fluid — for this, one needs *Bitul* / nullification of egoic rigidity. When we are water-like, we are able to make space for another to be birthed and to continue to become.

Laughter, and taking your sense of self 'lightly', creates a water-like quality. For example, Avraham and Sarah were already elderly and Sarah was barren. When it was revealed to them separately that they would miraculously have a child, each of them laughed: "And Avraham fell on his face and he laughed, and he said in his heart, 'Can a one hundred year old give birth' (*Bereishis*, 17:17). When Sarah heard,

"...Sarah laughed in her heart, and she said, after I am worn out and my lord is old, will I now have this pleasure" (*Ibid*, 18:12).

Whether their laugher was warranted or not, it served to break the tension between them and within them, and released them from their limited self-images. Ultimately, it allowed for the birth of new life. The laughter opened and empowered them to become vessels capable of receiving the Divine blessing of a child, and the Name of their child was thus Yitzchak, from the root word *Sechok* / laughter. (Rebbe Zusha of Anipoli teaches that 960 Lugin, plus 1 for the Mikvah itself, equal 961, which is the same numeric value as Avraham (248), Sarah (505), and their son, Yitzchak (208): 248+505+208 = 961).

A similar idea is found with regards to Dovid haMelech / King David. The Zohar calls Dovid "the King's jester" (*Zohar* 2, 107a). He was a person who was able to 'laugh' and take himself lightly in honor of Hashem's presence. We find that Dovid was acting in a 'light-hearted' way, dancing in front of the *Aron* / Ark which was being returned from captivity. He was overwhelmed with holy joy and did not take into consideration the personal dignity expected for his position of power. His wife Michal, the daughter of King Shaul, was upset about this, and she thought it was unbecoming for a king to act this way.

The verse says, "As the Ark of Hashem was entering the City of Dovid, Michal, the daughter of Shaul, watched from a window. When she saw Dovid haMelech leaping and dancing before Hashem, she despised him in her heart" (*Shemuel* 2, 6:16). At the end of the chapter, the verse concludes, "And Michal, the daughter of Shaul, had no children to the day of her death."

It appears from this textual juxtaposition as if Michal's inability to have children was some form of punishment for her criticizing Dovid haMelech's dancing. But if so, why such a harsh punishment, and why this specific punishment? What is the connection between her harsh disapproval of Dovid's perceived frivolity and her not bearing children?

Perhaps her barrenness was spiritually caused by her own lack of child-like sensitivity and spontaneity, which is a quality of water. She was unable to 'lower' herself like water, or become yielding like water, to accept her husband's behavior or respond to the moment in good faith. She was stuck in her narrative and inflexible in her definitions of appropriate decorum. She was unlike Avraham and Sarah who were able to laugh, to be light, vulnerable and selfless enough to open to the unexpected blessing of childbirth (See *Chagigah*, 5b).

Stepping into a Mikvah is stepping back into our own natural fluidity, the watery state we had before we became more rigid in our sense of self and expectations. This is the reason why a person who previously became angry must immerse in a Mikvah. An angry person is preoccupied with his self-image and importance; he does not currently know how to take himself lightly or 'fluidly'. Immersing in the waters of the Mikvah removes from us the burdens of our fixed self-image, returning us to a place of innocence and purity of intention.

CHAPTER 6

Kavanah / Intentions
when Immersing in the Mikvah

I N THIS CHAPTER, WE WILL EXPLORE THE DEEP-
ER CONNECTIONS BETWEEN VARIOUS PHYSICAL
DIMENSIONS OF THE MIKVAH and a series of Divine
Names in an attempt to further understand how the Mik-
vah can aid us in our process of energetic purification and
spiritual renewal.

Three Cosmic and Microcosmic Names

A simple observation reveals that a Mikvah contains three
basic dimensions: a) the floor you stand on when in the
Mikvah, B) the water that surrounds you — contained
within the four walls, and C) the water above your head, the
crown or roof of the Mikvah, when you are fully immersed.
Relatedly, in the Torah, there are three prominent Names
of Hashem:

> *HaVaYah* — the Yud-Hei-Vav-Hei, also called *Hashem*
> / the Name, or the Tetragrammaton. This name may be
> read or seen but not spoken
>
> *Ado-noi* — translated as "the L-rd". This is the name that
> we say in place of the Tetragrammaton. It is also some-
> times used as its own independent name.
>
> *Ehe'yeh* — "I am" or, more literally, "I will Be"; the Name
> which was revealed to Moshe at the Burning Bush.

Havayah represents ineffability and Infinity. The four letters, Yud-Hei-Vav-Hei, when rearranged, can spell out the
words *Hayah* (Hei-Yud-Hei), *Hovei* (Hei-Vav-Hei), *Yi'hi-*

yeh (Yud-Hei-Yud*-Hei) / 'Was, Is, Will Be'. The Name
Havayah thus represents the simultaneous totality of all
past, present and future — signifying infinite transcendence, beyond any conception of time.

The Name *Ado-noi* represents the Creator's mastery over
Creation. Today we pronounce the Name Havayah as *Ado-
noi*. This is because Ado-noi is like a garment or vessel in
which the totally transcendent Tetragrammaton vests itself in order to relate to the world of time and space. Ado-
noi is the receptacle and medium for Divine Immanence,
which allows for the utterly Transcendent Infinite One to
be experienced and expressed within Creation.** The Name
Ado-noi is the way Hashem's Presence presents itself in the
world today, and in this very moment.

Ehe'yeh is the Name related to the future, to 'becoming'. In
the Torah, the Name Ehe'yeh first appears to Moshe at the
Burning Bush. When Moshe encounters a bush aflame, yet
not consumed, he approaches and has a direct encounter
with the Divine. When he is told of his mission to free the
Children of Israel from Egypt, he asks, "When they ask me
what is His name, what should I tell them?" (*Shemos*, 3:13).

---

* In the Name of Hashem we can exchange the Vav for another Yud
  since Vav is understood as an elongated Yud.

** The Divine Name Ado-noi begins with an Aleph, alluding to Ehe'yeh,
   which begins with an Aleph, and the final letter is Yud, alluding to
   Havayah, which begins with a Yud. The middle letters, Dalet and Nun
   spell *Din* / judgment, limitation. *Rabbeinu Bachya*, Shemos, 4:28.

Here Moshe is asking for the highest Name to be revealed. The response he receives is, "Tell them *Ehe'yeh Asher Ehe'yeh*" sent you. This is often translated as, "I am That I am" but, more accurately this name means, "I will be, that which (or what) I will be." This implies, 'I will be with them now, in this hardship, and will also be with them in their future hardships' (*Rashi*, Shemos, 3:14). Additionally, this name also means: I am the 'I' that is expressed in everything — in the present as *Being*, and in the future as *Becoming*. The Ramban writes regarding this verse that *Ehe'yeh* is the Divine Name of the future, which is now known only to Hashem.

These are the three primary cosmic Names, correlating to three types of Divine 'expression' within this world — infinite transcendence or the beyond, immanent presence or being, and the future-oriented process of becoming. These names also have a microcosmic significance — an inner reality that reflects aspects of our own personal life.

Havayah is reflected as our root in infinite *Heviyah* / beingness prior to form. Since our souls are "a part of the Divine One Above, literally" (*Tanya*, 2), we each have a spark of Infinity within us. This sliver of the Infinite, as it were, has no definition or identity. It is free of all thoughts, feelings and impressions. It is pure, infinite potential, with no form or defined context, imageless and formless. It is the *Ayin* / emptiness, no-thing-ness 'before' *Yesh* / selfhood.

The Name Ado-noi, also conceptually referred to as *Adnus*, is our present ground of being, the reality that we are standing in right now relative to our current identity, thoughts, feelings and impressions. It is the fullness of our human lives as manifest within the stable and defined self-image we are inhabiting.

The Name *Ehe'yeh* is the infinite fullness of our potential in the ever-unfolding future that we are perpetually in the process of becoming.

Havayah — infinite root: 'backdrop': 'beyond'
Adnus — finite present / fruit: 'being'
Ehe'yeh — seed of infinite potential: 'becoming'

On the deepest level of Heviyah we are the formless and transparent experiencer of life, as opposed to a composite identity based on the impressions of our accumulated experiences or emotions. This is the backdrop of life, beyond the individual details of our personal stories. This is the pure space of awareness prior to experience which witnesses what is present and what is unfolding.

One practical way to 'immerse' and unify with this formless space of Heviyah is to deeply realize that whatever is able to be known cannot, by definition, be the knower. If you *know* your thoughts, then you cannot *be* your thoughts, you are that which knows. If you experience your passions, emotions and desires, this is proof that you are not them. These negations allow us to free ourselves from the limiting content of our experience, and reconnect us to the backdrop or context of life itself, back to the empty space in which all of life occurs and emerges from, including all our thoughts, emotions, actions, definitions and limitations. This space in itself is limitless, beyond all identification and conceptualization; infinite, as it were. This is the inner experience corresponding to the Name Havayah. Our deepest realization of this Name is perceiving the non-existence of our limited self.

The Name Ado-noi is reflected in the fullness of our human life. It is our self-image comprised of the thoughts we entertain, the words we speak, the actions we do, the emotions we feel and the impressions we accumulate. It is how we are manifesting ourselves in this life, for example, as a parent, child, spouse or sibling; as an artist, business person, doctor, lawyer or teacher, etc. It is, in short, our identity. All this and more is the range of experience symbolized by the Name Ado-noi. Our deepest realization of this Name is appreciating the Divine fullness that can enclothe itself within our present life and all its details.

And then there is our future self, our ever-unfolding process of infinite potential. Yesterday's becoming is today's being, and this divine aspect of infinite becoming gives us the ability to choose a tomorrow that will be radically different than today. This is the range of experience symbolized by the Name Ehe'yeh. Our deepest realization of this Name is believing in and acting on our unlimited potential.

NAME	DIMENSION OF EXPERIENCE	DIMENSION OF SELF	REALIZATION
Havayah	Primordial Backdrop 'Prior' to Experience	Your Inner Infinity	Perceiving the Emptiness of Self & Form
Adnus	Fullness of Present Experience	Your Garments of Finitude	Appreciating the Fullness of Self & Form
Ehe'yeh	Ever-Unfolding Process of Becoming	Your Infinite Potential or, Your Future Self	Believing in the Unlimited Potential of the Infinite

Three Names / Three Dimensions of the Mikvah

These three Divine Names — Hashem, Ado-noi, Ehe'yeh — are connected to the *Kavanos* / intentions of immersing in a Mikvah, as the Arizal explains (*Sha'ar Ruach haKodesh*, Yichud 77). Additionally, the Baal Shem Tov reveals further that these three Names, and the corresponding dimensions of our lives, are also reflected in the three dimensions of the

Mikvah: the floor, the water, and the 'roof' of the water. The floor is an expression of the Name Ado-noi, the water is an expression of the Name Havayah, and the roof of the water is an expression of Ehe'yeh (*Kedushas Levi,* Avos. *Baal Shem Tov, Torah,* Yisro, 11. Floor/Ado-noi, Water/Hashem, Roof/Ehe'yeh. Alternatively, Floor/Ado-noi, the person himself/Hashem, the entire water/Ehe'yeh. *Siddur Reb Shabtai,* p. 44. These three Names and dimensions of the Mikvah also correspond to *Dibbur* / speech, *Kol* / sound (the inner quality of speech), and *Machshavah* / thought, the root of sound and speech).

Floor — *Ado-noi*
Water — *Havayah (Hashem)*
Roof of the water — *Ehe'yeh*

The stable ground you stand upon when you are in the Mikvah represents Ado-noi. Personally and inwardly, this is the image you have of yourself in this present moment, comprised of all your thoughts, feelings, words and impressions that are 'creating' you as you are. The first thing you naturally do in the Mikvah, right before you immerse fully, is stand upright with your feet planted on the ground. This allows one's body and awareness to center and settle itself before immersing. Therefore, your first point of focus and intention is the floor you are standing on, and what it represents: your ground, your footing, your baseline, your standing in life and your self-definition.

The water that is swirling around you within the four walls of the Mikvah is a reflection of the Four Letter Name, Havayah. Water is unfixed and ungraspable, giving you a sense of infinity beyond all defined images or contextualizations.*

---

*The water in the Mikvah represents the Name of Hashem. More specifically, there are 4 possible ways to 'fill-out' the four letters (The Yud-Hei-Vav-Hei) in the Name of Hashem. For example, Hei can be spelled Hei Hei or Hei Yud, and so on for all the other letters in the Name. These four 'fillings' are known as the Names Av/72, Sag/63, Mah/45, Ban/52. There are a total of 9 Yuds in these four possibilities. (Av/72 is Yud (10) Vav (6) Dalet (4) = 20. Hei (5) Yud (10) = 15. Vav (6) Yud (10) Vav (6) = 22. Hei (5) Yud (10) = 15. In total is 72. Sag/63 is Yud (10) Vav (6) Dalet (4) = 20. Hei (5) Yud (10) = 15. Vav (6) Aleph (1) Vav (6) = 13. Hei (5) Yud (10) = 15. In total is 63. Mah/45 is Yud (10) Vav (6) Dalet (4) = 20. Hei (5) Aleph (1) = 6. Vav (6) Aleph (1) Vav (6) = 13. Hei (5) Aleph (1) = 6. In total is 45. Ban/52 is Yud (10) Vav (6) Dalet (4) = 20. Hei (5) Hei (5) = 10. Vav (6) Vav (6) = 12. Hei (5) Hei (5) = 10. In total is 52. In the Name Av there are 4 Yuds. In the Name Sag there are 3 Yuds. In the Name Mah there is 1 Yud, and in the Name Ban the Aleph is counted as one Yud, thus in total there are 9 Yuds). Yud is numerically 10, 9x10 = 90; this is the same as the numeric value of the word *Mayim* / water = 90 (*Reishis Chochmah*, Sha'ar haAhavah, 11. *Kanfei Yonah*, Sod haTevilah. Shaloh, *Sha'ar haOsyos*, Kuf, 8). The Name of Hashem is the Source and Creator of all reality. The very first letter to emerge in Creation was the letter Yud. (Aleph is the hidden 'first' letter of all letters.) The Yud therefore represents the potential of all other letters and the possibility of all manifestation and existence. Yud is the prima materia of all the other letters, as every letter in the Aleph-Beis, when written out, begins with a small letter Yud, a single point. Immersing in the 9 Yuds of the Name of Hashem means entering a place of pure creative potential.

Each side and wall of the Mikvah embodies another one of these four 'filled-out' Names of Hashem (*Pri Kodesh Hilulim*, Sha'ar Shabbos). The Name Av (72) is the east side. The Name Sag (63) is the north side. The Name Mah (45) is the south side. And the Name Ban (52) is the west side. Experientially, and in *Avodah* / personal service: one should think

So, as you begin to immerse, you move from a defined, static state of being, in which there is a strong image and sense of self, to a dynamic state under the water in which you are no longer a defined being or attached to a fixed self-image. At this point, you are completely free of negative images — in fact you are your Infinite self, without any images whatsoever.

When you stop identifying yourself *as* your thoughts, words or actions, you realize you are not angry, you are experiencing anger. You are thus not defined by this emotion. In this way, you are able to reconnect with the limitless potential of Ayin, the transcendent observer of all you experience, representing the infinite potential of self.

While under the water, you surrender all of your attachments to the finite, defined self that you work so hard at maintaining. In this fluid space, you are no longer defined by being a child, parent or spouse. Within the womb of

---

when facing inwardly east, to receive Divine wisdom and assume more purity; when facing north, to receive deeper understanding and learn more Torah; when facing south, to correct one's emotions and feel more love and awe of Hashem; and when facing west, to act more correctly and accept upon oneself the yoke of Heaven. Alternatively, the four walls represent the four letters in the Name *Ehe'yeh* and the waters themselves represent the Yud-Hei-Vav-Hei, and specifically the '72' Name in which each Hei spelled is with a Yud (Yud/Vav/Dalet. Hei/Yud. Vav/Yud/Vav. Hei/Yud). When you add 1 for the word itself, this adds up to a total numeric value of 73, which is the same as the word *Chochmah* / wisdom. *Pri Eitz Chayim*, Sha'ar haShabbos, 3.

the water you can experience a moment of Infinity, so to speak, and a total loss of attachment to finite life and its limitations. You are pure *Neshamah* / soul, which is a "part of the Divine, literally" (*Tanya*, Chap.2). You are one with the infinite awareness of pure Being.

Once submerged, the water's surface above your head, the roof through which you will emerge as you rise up from the Mikvah, is a reflection of the Name *Ehe'yeh.**

---

* In fact, *Ehe'yeh* spelled out, Aleph/1 + Lamed/30 + Pei/80 + Hei/5 + Hei/5 + Yud/10 + Vav/6, Dalet/4 + Hei/5 + Hei/5 = 151, has the same numeric value as the word *Mikvah*. The Kavanah for the Mikvah explained in the text is based on the teachings of the Arizal, the Baal Shem Tov and other similar sources. To fully decipher and comprehend the intricate details of the actual Kavanos of the Arizal, a good working understanding of the Arizal's teachings and system are necessary. Here is the first part of the original Kavanos of the Arizal (*Sha'ar haKavanos*, Leil Vav). Before immersion, have in mind that the Mikvah is the name Ehe'yeh spelled-out/filled-in as above: Aleph/1, Lamed/30, Pei/80 = 111, Hei/5-*Hei*/5 = 10, Yud/10, Vav /6, Dalet /4 = 20, and Hei /5-*Hei* / 5 = 10. In total is 151, same numeric value as Mikvah = 151. Afterwards, have in mind to draw down in this Mikvah "נחל / Nachal haElyon / the higher flow". These are the four ways (to spell/fill) the Name of Hashem mentioned in the previous note (in which the letters of the Name of Hashem are written out, equaling respectively (Av) 72 (Yud/10, Vav/6, Dalet/4 = 20. Hei/5, *Yud*/10 = 15. Vav/6, *Yud*/10, Vav/6 = 22. Hei/5, *Yud*/10 = 15. 20+15+22+15 = 72), (Sag) 63 (Yud/10, Vav/6, Dalet/4 = 20. Hei/5, *Yud*/10 = 15. Vav/6, *Aleph*/1, Vav/6 = 13. Hei/5, *Yud*/10 = 15. 20+15+13+15 = 63), (Mah) 45 (Yud/10, Vav/6, Dalet/4 = 20. Hei/5, *Aleph*/1 = 6. Vav/6, *Aleph*/1, Vav/6 = 13. Hei/5, *Aleph*/1 = 6. 20+6+13+6 = 45), and (Ban) 52 (Yud/10, Vav/6, Dalet/4 = 20. Hei/5, *Hei*/5 = 10. Vav/6, Vav/6 = 12. Hei/5, *Hei*/5 = 10. 20+10+12+10 = 52), and the three 'fillings' of the Name Ehe'yeh with Yuds (as in Hei-Yud) or with Alephs (as in Hei-Aleph) or with Heis (as above). In these seven names (in their simple, basic four letter spelling, Yud-Hei-Vav-Hei and Aleph-Hei-Yud-Hei) there are seven Yuds, a Yud in each name.

This is the portal through which the new you, the possible you, the future you, will be born.

We cannot live under water, as it were, or exist in this world with no sense of finite identity. Your purpose is not simply to remain within the womb of the infinite, and to thereby let go of acting in the world and using your special talents. If, for example, you find yourself in the role of 'a good lawyer', then be a good lawyer and do good things with your practice and your money. Just do not get too *caught up* in this finite image of yourself to the extent that you forget who you truly are — an infinite Neshamah which is a part of Hashem. As you are working in the world, always remember the *Tachlis* / ultimate purpose of your life.

Our purpose is not to simply be our infinite self, and let go of all images, not utilizing our special talents. Rather, it is

---

These seven Names are the secret of the seven Names of Shabbos and the seven letters of the Names Ehe'yeh (4 letters) and Yud-Hei-Vav (3 letters). One needs to have in mind, in addition to these seven Yuds, the complete filling of these (two) names. Add the Name Yud-Hei (2 letters), which is the secret of Shabbos, thus there are now eight Yuds. Yud is numerically 10. Eight Yuds = 80, these correspond to the נל of נחל. Nun is 50, Lamed is 30 = 80, and with the eight (eight is the letter Ches) you have the word נחל. *Nachal* numerically is thus 88, with the two types of Yuds (seven from the four possible ways to write out the Yud-Hei-Vav-Hei and the three ways to write out Aleph-Hei-Yud-Hei. And the one Yud from Yud-Hei), the total is 90, the numeric value of the word *Mayim* / water. Thus, have intention that the Mayim (which is equivalent to the above Divine Names) is being drawn into the Mikvah in which you are now going to immerse yourself.

to emerge from the Mikvah to go back into the world and return with a "positive" image of self. As you are emerging from the formless waters of the Mikvah, you must re-invest your infinite potential within a pure, new image of self with a positive purpose in the world. For this reason, the *Teharah* / purity created by means of the Mikvah only occurs as we emerge from the water and move back into the world. This new Yesh is the ultimate objective of our immersion into the waters of Ayin (*Kesef Mishnah*, Rambam *Hilchos Avos haTumah*, 6:16. *Tosefos*, Shabbos, 35a, *v'Yarad*). Moving back into the world is the objective of the Mikvah immersion.

The complete process of *Tevilah* / immersion is composed of two elements: submerging under the water and emerging from the water. As explored, these two elements correspond to the Names Havayah and Ehe'yeh. The word *Tovel* / immerse (Tes/9, Vav/6, Beis/2, Lamed/30) is numerically 47, the same numeric value as the Names Ehe'yeh (21) and Hashem (26) combined (*Toras Levi Yitzchak*, Mikvaos). Thus, to Tovel is to meditate on and unify these two names.

As explored, Mikvah literally means 'a place of gathering'. This does not only refer to a gathering of waters, but more deeply, it implies a gathering of your entire self, your *Adnus*, within the water. In fact, not a single strand of hair should remain outside the water. Similarly, not a single element of our past, present or potential future should remain outside of our awareness. We gather, own and unify with our past; we embrace our entire narrative, so that we can let all of it go in the *Havayah* of the water. Having released it and having seen its emptiness for what it truly is, we can faithfully emerge through the water's roof of *Ehe'yeh* into a brighter future.

Hachna'ah, Havdalah, Hamtakah

According to the Baal Shem Tov, every transformation and successful leap of progress demands three steps: 1) *Hachna'ah* / submission, then 2) *Havdalah* / separation, and finally 3) *Hamtakah* / sweetening. We will explore this paradigmatic process in relation to the Mitzvah, and experience of, Mikvah.

Hachna'ah

Hachna'ah is the humbling stage of submission and acceptance. This is the process of looking honestly at your life up until this present moment and fully acknowledging and embracing all of yourself as you are. This includes not only your body, identity, status, thoughts and feelings, but also all of your past mistakes and shortcomings. Hachna'ah is to humbly accept all aspects of yourself as your own doing, and part of your being. Who you are in this moment is the sum total of the ways you have been manifesting yourself in the world up to this point.

Performing a *Cheshbon haNefesh* / accounting of the soul

is the first step in Mikvah immersion. This is the spiritual in-gathering and owning of your own life, however uncomfortable it may be. This internal process is analogous to the physical experience of stepping into and finding your footing on the floor of the Mikvah. The submission of Hachna'ah is to acknowledge who and where you are at, in the present moment, as well as what your current ground of being is: your 'floor', your *Adnus*.

Honest assessment and acknowledgment of who we are, and how we got here, is required for us to move on in a meaningful way. This is because we cannot forget, let go of and move beyond that which do not remember. We therefore must begin our Mikvah immersion by contemplating our 'floor' level of being. As you stabilize yourself on the ground of the Mikvah, think about where you are in the course of your life. While standing in the water, before immersing, ask yourself: 'What type of thoughts do I have most regularly? Are my thoughts holy and positive, or are they unholy and self-defeating? Are my thoughts genuinely liberating and inspiring, or are they riddled with doubts and anxieties?'

Continue in this manner: Are the words you speak holy, meaningful, helpful — or the opposite: hateful, spiteful, or even just wasteful? Do you use refined or crass language? Do you speak with gentleness or do you scream?

How about your actions? What are you doing with your life? Are your actions healthy, just, life-affirming — or the opposite? Does the way you live your life on a daily basis express or contradict your highest values?

How are you manifesting yourself in the world? Are you presenting yourself as a person with anger issues? A holy person? What is the impact you're making as a parent, daughter, son or friend? Let these questions allow for a deeper level of self-awareness to emerge as you step into the Mikvah and sense the Ado-noi, the ground, of your own life. This is the gift of Hachna'ah: To humbly acknowledge and embrace all of yourself, with all of your achievements and aspirations, faults and failings.

Now we will slowly move beneath the surface of the waters of the Mikvah.

Havdalah

Feel the sacred waters surrounding your body, embracing you and holding you. Lift your feet gently off the ground and become one with the flow around you. Let go! Unburden yourself of all that you're so desperately holding on to. Let the image of your small self dissolve like a dewdrop in the Infinite ocean of Hashem's love; release all of your limited definitions and limiting expectations into the *Havayah* of the water.

Allow the living waters of purity to uplift you, making you completely weightless. You are empty, luminous, free, energized; everything is possible. You have no fixed Tzurah; you are a watery embryo swimming within the womb of the Creator. You are cradled in Infinite, Silent Light, floating free from all binding elements of identity, image, thought, feeling, action, worry, doubt, negativity. You are a pure, sparkling Neshamah blending back into the Source of Being.

Under the water, in a state of Havdalah, you have achieved total transcendence of your entire manifest life; you are detached from your body, your personality, your past and your struggles. You understand in this moment that you are not anything that you have ever done; you are not your thoughts, nor your emotions. Yes, you have 'had' emotions, feelings, thoughts; but in fact, you never 'were' them. Your Neshamah has a body, but you are not your body.

From this place of Havdalah, you are ready to reemerge from the water and rejoin Creation, individuality and your body, in a graceful and grateful way. It is time to be reborn.

Hamtakah

Slowly return your feet to the floor again, and move your body upward until your face and head gently part the transparent roof of the waters. As you take your first breath in this new life, feel the relief and invigoration it brings you.

Your breath is a gift, given to you at just the right moment, with great love, care, pride and faith in who you are. As more of your form is birthed from the water, feel how your skin glistens like that of the First Human Being awakening in Gan Eden. Your body and mind are new, full of light and energy. Life is full of potential and hope. A smile of gratitude blossoms deep within you for this Hamtakah / sweetening of all reality.

Leaving behind the fluid non-identity of the infinite Ayin state, you have successfully passed through the birth canal of the Name Ehe'yeh with a renewed sense of becoming. As you ascend the Mikvah steps, you are the living embodiment of a healthy, holy, positive image of yourself. You realize that from now on, you can live and act in this world with a deeply ingrained sense of *Hecherkeit* / elevation and nobility. You feel as though you will never forget or lose focus on who you truly are, a pure Neshamah — an intimate part of the Infinite entrusted with a Divine mandate, a vital mission and unique purpose.

In the course of these three steps, you have moved from negative, ego-based attachments of self and identity, down into a state of complete non-attachment to all form, and finally up into a holy reintegration into form. Clearly, this third level of Hamtakah could not have been achieved without stage two, Havdalah, and similarly you could not have achieved real Havdalah without first experiencing

Hachna'ah. Each stage is thus both necessary and also meant to be transcended in an infinite spiral of spiritual growth and development.

Stage of Transformation	Physical Movement	Dimension of Mikvah	Divine Name	Contemplation
1 **Hachna'ah**	Standing in Mikvah	Floor	Ado-noi	Humbly accepting your life as it is
2 **Havdalah**	Immersing in Water	Water within the four walls of Mikvah	Havayah	Transcending or, letting go of your past life
3 **Hamtakah**	Emerging from Water	Surface of Water	Ehe'yeh	Coming alive again

Yichud / Unification,
Beracha / Blessing,
Kedushah / Holiness

When added together, these three names, Ado-noi, Hashem and Ehe'yeh, equal 112. (*Ado-noi:* Aleph/1 + Dalet/4 + Nun/50 + Yud/10 = 65. *Havayah:* Yud/10 + Hei/5 + Vav/6 + Hei/5 = 26. *Ehe'yeh:* Aleph/1 + Hei/5 + Yud/10 + Hei/5 = 21. Finally, 26 + 65 + 21 = 112.) The number 112 is also the value of the sacred Name of Hashem called *YaBoK* (Yud/10 + Beis/2 + Kuf/100 =112. *Pri Eitz Chayim*, 1, Sha'ar 17, Keriyas Shema she'al haMita, 10. Sha'ar 17, Tikkun Chatzos, 3).

After years of travel and toil while running away from his brother Esav, building a large family and amassing an abundance of wealth outside the Promised Land of Israel in the process, Yaakov finally returns to Israel after 22 years. *Yabok* is the Name of the river which Yaakov crossed over upon entering Israel before he encountered his brother Esav. Significantly, the two names Yaakov and Yabok are comprised of the very same letters, alluding to the fact that Yaakov's crossing of the Yabok was a transformative experience that revealed new aspects of his being.

Deeper still, the three letter Name *YaBoK* is an acronym for *Yichud* / Unity, **Beracha** / Blessing, and **Kedushah** / holiness. In order to reemerge from the waters as a new you — with the power of the Name *Ehe'yeh* — to become a healthier, more positive image of yourself and reconnect with your life's purpose, you must perform Hachna'ah in relation to your identity. Submit to the facts of your own life: 'Yes, I am a child of so-and-so, a spouse of so-and-so — I accept these realities as building blocks of my identity. This is my body, these are my circumstances, this is what I do, this is how I speak, this is how I think, *this is my life.*' In this way, compassionately create a full picture of your experience in this world, your social standing and persona, your financial advantages or disadvantages, your state of health, your relationships, your past choices, your pains and your pleasures. This Hachna'ah will allow you to make an existential *Yichud* (the Yud of *YaBoK*) — to unify the entire context of your life and all its details, including every act you have done, and everything that has happened to you without your choice. This integration of all aspects of yourself and your story, of your past and purpose, is the first necessary step in completing one phase of your journey, in order to begin the next.

Then, after a full unification and acceptance of your past and personality, make a Havdalah with your life. Step back from this entire edifice of identity and view yourself as if you were another person, not-you. Often we are so entangled with our day-to-day concerns, that, even if we can 'own' our life through Hachna'ah, we still cannot see all of it with complete objectivity. This is why it is easier for us to notice another person's blessings, talents and opportunities; we are our own blindspot. With Havdalah, initiating a temporary separation from your subjective point of view, you are able to see and appreciate the many blessings occurring in the backdrop, or space, of your life. You can see your whole life as one continuous Berachah (the Beis of *YaBoK*).

In truth, your whole life *is* a blessing because everything that happens brings you closer to Hashem and to your ultimate purpose. The reason you have that family, that body with all its traits, that birthplace, etc., is that through this precise context, your Neshamah can achieve its maximum Tikkun. And this is what brings you to Kedushah (the Kaf of *YaBoK)* — to closeness with Hashem and living your purpose. Whatever exists for you is what brings you to What Is, or What Will Be. This realization is the Hamtakah of your life.

By immersing in the Mikvah according to the three stages of transformation, as taught by the Baal Shem Tov, you are able to emulate Yaakov as he crossed the Yabok on his way home to the Promised Land. Along the way, you must create a Yichud with the entire environment and context of your life through Hachna'ah; recognize that all of it is a blessing through Havdalah; and understand deeply that every experience and obstacle is an opportunity to achieve Kedushah, and manifest your holy mission on earth.

From this perspective, even the negative choices you have made in life can drive you to make more positive choices in the present and future, if processed productively. In fact, when they do ultimately bring you to positive deeds, your past mistakes are redeemed, and their energy is sweetened. With genuine *Teshuvah* / self-transformation, past malice is turned into merit, and everything in life can be felt as the Berachah, source of blessing, it truly is. For the greatest blessing and sweetness in life is being on a path of Kedushah.

Yud of the Name *YaBoK*	Yichud	Hachna'ah	Adnus	Floor of Mikvah
Beis of the Name *YaBoK*	Berachah	Havdalah	Havayah	Water of Mikvah
Kuf of the Name *YaBoK*	Kedushah	Hamtakah	Ehe'yeh	Roof of Water

In summary:

The inner work of Hachna'ah (and Yichud) should start as you are walking to the Mikvah, or at least as you are taking a moment to stand firmly on the floor of the Mikvah before you immerse. Think about your life and own it.

Then, as you are lowering yourself in the water, practice Havdalah: 'I am not my thoughts, feelings, words or actions. I am not my body. I am one with the Infinite One, formless and full of potential blessing.'

As your head is slowly emerging from the waters, see that your whole life, from beginning to end, is a blessing (Beracha). And now as you emerge fully from the Mikvah with a healthy, wholesome sense of self, go on to follow your path of deepest Kedushah. This is the ultimate sweetening of all prior judgments.

Now, like Yaakov, you have followed your path through the Mikvah* of YaBoK, moving forward with your life, and entering the inner Promised Land. You are now ready to encounter all struggles head-on with confidence, focus and determination — and ultimately, victory. You are now ready for redemption.

---

* The first time in the Torah that the word Mikvah appears is in the *Pasuk* / verse "ולמקוה המים קרא ימים" / and the gathering of the waters, He called seas" (*Bereishis*, 1:10). The Arizal teaches (*Sha'ar Ruach haKodesh*, p. 36. *Sha'ar haKavanos* 2, p. 25) that the first letters of each of these four words (Vav/6, Hei/5, Kuf/100, Yud/10) add up to 121. The number 121 is equivalent to the Four Letter Name of Hashem / 26 (Yud-Hei-Vav-Hei) plus the five letter Name *Elokim* (aleph-lamed-hei-yud-mem) 86 = 112. Hashem has 4 letters and Elokim has five, thus the total number is 121. And 112 is the value of the Name *YaBoK*. One should have this in mind before immersing in a Mikvah. Specifically, you can have in mind what this process of YaBoK facilitates and represents within us, and how we are entering into the primordial Mikvah — the original Mikvah — of Creation. According to *Maor Einayim* when entering a Mikvah one should meditate on these words, and specifically, how the first letters of these four words numerically equals 121, similar to how the five letter Name Elokim (86), and the four letter Name Hashem (26), plus the 9 letters from these two names = 121; this represents a constricted mind-state. Additionally, one should also meditate on how through the immersion, one gains a level of elevated expansiveness. In the Mikvah, instead of the water being spread out (as at the beginning of creation), the water becomes gathered, revealing fresh and fertile ground for growth: "And G-d called the dry land earth"; now, from this place of renewed creation, new blessings can manifest.

The Delight of Sweetening

When a person moves inwardly from Hachna'ah to Ha-vdalah, and eventually to Hamtakah, it generates great joy and inner *Oneg* / pleasure and delight. Completing this three-tier process, you feel a sense of completeness and genuine peace; you are whole again.

Numerically, the value of the word *Oneg* (Ayin/70 + Nun/50 + Gimel/2) is 123, and with the word itself, is 124. This is also the value of the word *Eden* / pleasure, the home of the primordial garden. The value of the Names Ado-noi (65), Havayah (26) and Ehe'yeh (21), plus the 12 letters (each of these Names contain 4 letters) also equals 124 (*Kehilas Yaakov*, Erech Oneg). Oneg is achieved when we unify our life, when everything of our past can be seen as a blessing, and when we are empowered from the deepest resources and potentials of our soul to become who we truly desire to become. When we own our life, and then let go of it in the Mikvah of Hashem, we can emerge whole again, with a new lease on life and with great joy and pleasure.

Recreation of Self

Mikvah has the same letters as the word *Kumah* / uplift (*Tikunei Zohar*, p. 37b. *Baal Shem Tov*, Torah, Yisro 11. *Degel Machanei Ephrayim*, Likutim, 252). A Mikvah uplifts a person and helps establish the spiritual/energetic foundation for a more elevated life. In the language of Chazal, the measurement of a Kosher Mikvah is a pool of water "in which one's entire body is *Olah* / elevated". As we learned previously, the word *Olah* here is understood to mean 'immersed' (*Eiruvin*, 4b), yet literally it means 'elevated'. This is because when we emerge from the purifying waters of the Mikvah, we are uplifted (Kumah) and elevated (Aliyah) into a new life. Parenthetically, a Mikvah that becomes unkosher for use is called *Yored* / degraded (*Makos*, 3b), and it does not elevate us.

When we *Tovel* / immerse, nullify our *Yeshus* / ego and arrogance, and experience *Bitul* / nullification, we become connected to the World of *Ayin* / emptiness, which is also referred to as *Keser* / Crown. A crown is worn above the head, alluding to the most elevated level of consciousness. Keser is a Divine space which is above and unaffected by any human thoughts or actions. From Keser we can draw down a new *Kumah* / structure and can start life over again (Tzemach Tzedek, *Sefer haLikutim*, Mikvah, p. 1461). *Tevilah* / immersion is numerically 57 (with the word itself), which is the same value as the words *Hu Adam* / this is a human being (Shaloh, *Sha'ar haOsyos*, 12). Through immersion in the Mikvah we became a true human, a holy, elevated and upright being capable of consciously connecting to the Divine. This experience of recreation naturally calls forth gratitude and a desire to give honor to the sacredness and transformative power of the Mikvah. There are, therefore, those who have a custom to leave the waters of the Mikvah walking backwards, facing the water, as if leaving the presence of a teacher or a *Shul* / synagogue (Shaloh, *Sha'ar haOsyos*, Kedushah, 9. *Kanfei Yonah*, 3:45). Even if this is not your custom, you should still focus on taking leave of the Mikvah with conscious intention and level-headedness, with respect and mindfulness. Certainly, we should not quickly jump or run out of the Mikvah "the way a child runs away when he is let out of school" (*Tosefos*, Shabbos, 116a. *Ramban*, Bamidbar, 10:35), as this shows that we just want the experience to be over. When we leave the Mikvah with awareness it shows our appreciation for the process, our honor of the Mikvah, and our understanding of the magnitude of what has just transpired.

THREE PRACTICAL
KAVANOS / INTENTIONS
FOR THE MIKVAH

KAVANAH ONE

~~~

Removing Garments

THIS IS AN ELABORATION ON THE HISPASHTUS KAVANAH, PROVIDED ABOVE. The basis of this practice is the important psychological and spiritual principle of "The heart is drawn after the actions" (*Sefer haChinuch*, Mitzvah 16). What we do physically with our bodies stimulates an analogous response within our consciousness.

To enter a Mikvah, we must first remove all our clothing, as there should be no *Chatzitzah* / separation between our bodies and the water. Any external appendage or attachment that can be removed from the body, such as jewelry or makeup, must be removed before immersion. In this way, the tangible sense of *Hishpashtus* / divestment of our materiality while being under water, extends logically and practically to the act of removing one's garments. The process of taking off each garment creates a visceral sensation of letting go, a sense of peeling away the layers covering and concealing your real self.

How we remove garments, and also how we get dressed, have a deep inner impact and demand mindfulness and intention. For example, even when we are in a hurry, we should not take off two garments at once (*Shulchan haTohar*, (Kamarna), Orach Chayim, 2:1. Others argue that this only refers to *putting on* two garments at once). This lack of mindfulness or impatience can be a root cause of *Shich'cha* / forgetfulness.

To begin, as you are entering the room to remove your garments before immersion, think about how the physical act of undressing stimulates your sense of taking account and letting go, acknowledging each covering individually before removing it.

Next, we should start undressing from the left side of our body; for example, remove the left shoe before the right shoe (*Shabbos*, 61a. *Shulchan Aruch haRav*, 2:4. There are differing customs for left-handed people; in general their left is considered their right and so they reverse the sides given in these instructions.). Even within each garment, we ought to begin by removing the left side first; for example, the left leg of the pants, and then the right (see *Aruch haShulchan*, Orach Chayim, 2:7). The left side represents one's weaker side, and is thus more connected to the world of *Din* / judgment and constriction. It is appropriate to first remove the side corresponding to this energy, so as to be free from it earlier in the process.

There is also another practice to undress progressing from below to above (*Derech Eretz Zuta*, 8. See however, *Derech Eretz*, 10, where it implies one is to get undressed from top to bottom, as the Kohanim, *Yuma*, 25a, and later dress from the bottom garments to the top. This was the custom of Ashkenaz, and the general custom when dressing a deceased body. *Gesher haChayim*, 10:2). In addition, one usually removes all outer garments before their undergarments. Therefore, we have three elements to the sequence: taking off garments from left to right, from below to above, and from outer to inner.

Removing Shoes

Begin by removing your shoes and socks, then move to your pants, skirt or dress, and finally to the garments on the upper part of the body, concluding with your head covering. This sequence is also symbolic of beginning with what is *Kal* / easy and progressing to what is more *Kaved* / difficult. That is, it can be easier to let go of overt negativity in your 'lower' elements or actions, than it is to let go of the more subtle, perhaps more deceptive negativities residing in your higher faculties, such as your feelings, words and thoughts. When taking off your shoes, begin with your left shoe, then your right shoe. Shoes suggest mastery. As you are taking off your shoes, let go of your assumed mastery over your life. Let go of the need to be in control, and give control over to Hashem. This will help you strengthen your faith and have more *Bitachon* / trust in the Master of the Worlds.

When you let go of controlling your surroundings, you can let go of anxiety and worries. These are emotions that rise up because we feel that we can rule over our own future. Based on our estimation of how our life is unfolding, we may decide we are moving into a future riddled with anxiety, uncertainty and reason to worry. Maybe your job does not seem to pay enough to put your children through school, or to buy a home, or to retire. Maybe it seems to you that everything that is going on with your spouse and children, with your livelihood or health, is solely dependent on you. Or maybe there is another specific situation in your life from which you do not see a way out based on your current circumstances or limitations. When you remove your shoes, let them drop to the ground, along with your grasping for control; drop your worries and sense in your bare feet the holy vulnerability of trusting in Hashem.

Taking off your shoes releases you from the need to feel like the master of the world.

Let the One who guides your every step lead you along the path of liberation and inner redemption.

Removing Lower Garments

The pants or skirt covering the lower part of the body is the garment that 'hide one's shame'. After Adam and Chavah / Eve ate from the Tree of Knowledge, they became painfully self-aware: "And they knew that they were naked, and they sewed fig leaves and made themselves *Chagoros* / girdles" (*Bereishis*, 3:7). This is a type of belt that is worn at the waist and covers the lower part of the body.

Garments that cover the lower parts of the body represent the ability to interact with the world while simultaneously covering the shame or secret one harbors within. A higher and deeper way of living a spiritual life is to live without shame. However, people often do want to fit in, and not to stand out as different, because they are ashamed of what others might think about them. Because of this, they may not act in the world according to the ways they really want to, this may be the case with regard to physical, monetary, relationship, job, creative or spiritual pursuits.

Shame can be crippling. When it overwhelms a person it can lead to a kind of self-imprisonment, preventing confident, courageous and necessary actions. For such a person, confusion ensues between what they feel they 'have' to do, what they 'want' to do, and deeper still what their soul is telling them to do.

"*Be bold as a leopard*...means that one should not to be ashamed when confronted by a scoffer" (*Avos*, 5:20. *Shulchan Aruch*, Orach Chayim, 1:1). We must strive to live with conviction, to know what we need to do in this world and do it proudly. We cannot let the scoffers of the world, those who are jealous, those who cannot bear to see another person's success, take us down.

In the place of shame, we can cultivate the positive quality of empowered humility, which is a healthy balance achieved between the Sefiros of Hod and Netzach, and embodied in the legs. With this firm footing, we can step forward and act in the world simply because it is the right thing to do.

As you remove your lower external garments,
drop any assumed need to hide or be embarrassed.

Be free of shame.

Embrace the holy humility that empowers and inspires you
to live your truth in a compassionate way.

Removing Upper Garments

Your shirt conceals and protects your heart, the place of
your yearnings, emotions, hopes and dreams. The heart can
be alive to our deepest desire, our yearning to sense a closeness with Hashem — or it can want what is not good for
us and what does not belong to us, *Chas veShalom* / Heaven
forbid. Our hearts can be filled with love for the deeper life
of Torah and Mitzvos, or filled with self-destructive lust
and fear.

The heart is the place of emotional investments and attachments, whether holy or mundane. An unrefined heart is
attached to insatiable, irrational desires such as for power,
honor or fleeting pleasure. Such negative attachments are
Kelipos / encrustations, which constrict and dull the heart
by diverting the vital energy of passionate emotion into
self-centered nonsense.

As you remove your upper external garments, release your

heart from any of its constricting shells.

Breathe deeply as all attachments to egoic desire, arrogance and fear drop away.

Removing Undergarments

Next, as you are taking off your inner, more intimate garments, let go of all your thoughts and personal expressions, to the best of your ability. Stop following any thoughts about the past or future, and just be present. As you have dropped your external garments on the bench or chair, or hung them on a hook, and no longer carrying their weight, sense that you are no longer carrying the burden of your constricting or unnecessary internal garments and Kelipos.

Your Neshamah is free and unencumbered.

Feel the lightness of your being, there is nothing weighing you down any longer, as all external and negative attachments have been removed. You are quite literally in a state of Hispashtus. In this state, calmly descend the steps into the water. Do not rush or jump in (Rambam, *Hilchos Mikvaos,* 1:9, as it may appear that one is simply jumping in to cool down, *Teshuvas haRivash, Keseph Mishnah* ad loc). Notice how the water receives you completely, allowing you to release the weight of your body, and even your sense of being a separate individual.

You stand prepared to immerse into the water, where you will be totally free, reabsorbed into Infinity.

You are at this moment a transparent, empty vessel ready to receive Hashem's blessings of Kedushah and Teharah. Ready to be refreshed and begin anew.

KAVANAH TWO

~~~

Immersing in the Mikvah

WHAT FOLLOWS IS A FURTHER ELABORATION OF THE PRACTICAL KAVANOS FOR IMMERSION DESCRIBED EARLIER.

As you are standing in the waters of the Mikvah, feet planted on the ground, think about who you are in the present moment. This first step corresponds to the Name Ado-noi, the ground of being, the finite foundation of your life, and of the created world at large.

Ask yourself: What is the state my life? How am I expressing myself in this world? What am I doing with my time? Acknowledge your ground of being, where you are holding, for better or worse, physically, emotionally, mentally and spiritually. Be honest and compassionate.

Own your life. Remember: this is 'your' life; these are your mistakes, your habits, your beliefs, your successes. This is your body, your instrument and vessel. These are your parents, siblings, children, spouse, friends, co-workers, community, circumstances and choices.

Practice Hachna'ah; acknowledge and accept the situation that you are in, whatever it may be.

Now, slowly, enter more fully into the waters, and sense the waters receiving you unquestioningly.

As your body submerges, take notice of the water enveloping you on all four sides, corresponding to the Four Letter Ineffable Name, Yud-Hei-Vav-Hei. You are embraced in Hashem's open arms, as it were. "The Mikvah of Israel is Hashem" — sense the fullness of Hashem's unconditional love for you.

Notice the contrast between the solidity of the floor beneath you, and the soft, swirling waters around you.

Step deeper into the Mikvah and immerse yourself completely in the water, lifting off the stable ground beneath you, into the boundless fluidity surrounding you. You are weightless, no longer attached to any finite images or narratives of yourself, your circumstances, your challenges or even your body.

Stay underneath the water for a moment, a little longer than would be natural. As you are under the water think of how you are truly beyond nature, one with the Infinite One. You are full of endless, supernatural potential.

Dip into and out of the water. With each immersion feel yourself as more and more emptied, open and free.

During your immersions, consider focusing on one or more of these Kavanos:

I am clear of all Tumah, free from all Kelipah, empty of all form. Now...

I want to accept upon myself the commitment to become a deeper person,

A person who lives for a higher purpose beyond the fulfillment of my own desires.

I want to pray with more Kavanah.

I want to learn more Torah.

I want to learn Torah with more enthusiasm

I want to be more charitable, more sensitive and responsive to the needs of others.

I want to be a better husband, wife, child, parent, sibling, friend.

I want to live my life with a more revealed connection to Hashem.

I want to be more mindful, more present in each and every moment.

I want to live with less stress and more trust in Hashem.

I want to feel my emotions deeply and honestly without being consumed by them.

I want to think, speak and act in rectified and righteous ways, not out of lust, despondency or craving for honor.

～～

This is just a general list of suggested intentions to keep in mind while immersing in the Mikvah. However, every person should think deeply about what areas in life they personally need to correct, and where they might need to obtain support and encouragement.

Now, in your concluding immersion, as you are about to pass through the surface of the waters, focus silently on the Name Ehe'yeh. As you break through, and are reborn, feel your in-breath filling you. Realize that all Tumah and negativity has been washed away, and that you have a completely open potential to manifest your new future in a holy, healthy and integrated way.

As you step away from the Mikvah, turn to face the waters and take a couple steps backwards, as if leaving a Shul or *Rebbe* / spiritual teacher — alternatively, you may honor the spiritual gift of Mikvah inwardly without turning around.

Express gratitude in your heart for the fact that you have been cleansed, and are now re-entering the world with a deeper sense of *Yichud* / unity, *Berachah* / blessing, and *Kedushah* / purity.

KAVANAH THREE

Getting Redressed

BEFORE YOU ENTERED INTO THE MIKVAH YOU HAD RELEASED AND UNBURDENED YOURSELF FROM THE WEIGHT and constriction of all garments and attachments. Now is the time to re-collect your garments and re-dress as a new person with new garments, as it were. Now you are ready to re-encounter the world enclothed in a new level of holiness, purity, freshness and aliveness.

While the common practice is to undress from below to above, as explored previously, the sequence in getting re-dressed, starts from the top-down, putting on upper-body garments first and lower-body garments last (R. Meir Papiras, *Ohr Tzadikim*, 1), concluding with the shoes.

Now you are fully adorned, girded and ready to enter the world anew. With the protection of your rectified garments, no negativity can harm you. It should be noted that if you are getting dressed after the Mikvah on Erev Shabbos, there is a custom to say or think the verse, "Any weapon whetted against you shall not succeed..." (*Yeshayahu*, 54:17. Shaloh, *Sha'ar haOsyos*, Kedushah, 9. *Kanfei Yonah*, 3:45). This, again, is another expression of the fundamental idea of being dressed in 'new' garments of purity and holiness which serve to protect and shield you from all negativity, distraction and diversion from truth and wholeness.

CHAPTER 7

Mikvah for Women

THE ESSENTIAL MITZVAH OF MIKVAH TODAY IS ASSOCIATED WITH MARRIED WOMEN; all other practices of immersion are communal customs or spiritual practices, as explored previously. Within the rhythm of a marriage, there are times in the month when a couple may be physically intimate, and there are times when they must refrain from physical contact.

Without getting into all the details of these intricate laws, during menstruation and the following seven 'clean' days, spouses need to be physically separate, and before they can be intimate again, the wife must immerse in a Mikvah. Until a woman (whether married or single) who has menstruated immerses herself in a Mikvah, she is called a Nidah. In this chapter, we will explore some of the deeper aspects of intimacy and how the Mikvah can help us achieve a holy and pure union on all levels.

As the Ramban writes: The act of intimacy can be the holiest and purest action in the world (*Iggeres haKodesh* attributed to the Ramban, 2. *Ramban* on Shemos, 30:13. See however, Rambam, *Moreh Nevuchim*, 3:8 and *Sefer haChinuch*, Mitzvah 117). When approached with Kavanah, with mindfulness, tenderness and holiness, and, as the Zohar adds, when performed with *Achdusa* / unity, *Chedvasa* / joy, and *Reusa* / desire, it can be a physical act that embodies the deepest quality in the world: genuine unity (*Zohar* 3, 7a. Note *Kidushin*, 41a. Rambam, *Hilchos Ishus*, 15:17). When done correctly, it can be a glimmer of the World to Come, a glimpse into the Ultimate Reality of Infinite Unity (although, see *Berachos*, 57b).

Hashem's Presence, the essence and root of all *Yichud* / oneness, rests between spouses who are cleansed and pure on all levels (*Sotah*, 17a). In the words of the holy Zohar, "The Divine Presence rests upon the marital space when spouses are united in love and holiness." The *Koach* / power of *Ein Sof* / Infinity is revealed within this earthly Yichud, as expressed in the power to emulate the Creator and create a new child.

Indeed, every time there is a Yichud, when two bodies are unified as one, *Neshamos* / souls are created. Physical intimacy, even if it doesn't result in bodily pregnancy, creates souls. 'Souls', in this context, means spiritual vibrations, flows and energies, as well as an emotional and mental atmosphere, an ambiance that hovers over and rests between the spouses. Yet, it is only with actual physical unity, that bona-fide *Neshamos* / souls, not just holy vibrations, are generated, as the Tzemach Tzedek explains.

However, every holy union creates positive spiritual *Chayus* / energy, vitality, flow that affects all worlds, above and below. In fact, even when two people just communicate deeply with each other, baring and sharing themselves and connecting with each other on a deep and vulnerable level, a 'third entity', a new dimension of spirituality, is created and revealed in the world.

When there is a level of *Neshikin* / kisses, for example, *Malachim* / angels are created. The kisses below, which are a unity of mind and heart, ripple through all worlds and create a corresponding mental and emotional energy, giving birth to an ethereal angel. When, however, there is body-to-body connection, essence-to-essence intimacy, souls are birthed. An essence-to-essence communion on this plane of reality is a mirror image of the unity of the essence of self with the *Etzem* / Essence of Hashem, the root of all Souls (Tzemach Tzedek, *Derech Mitzvosecha*, Mitzvah Peru uRevu).

Therefore, every act of physical intimacy, whether or not it actually produces physical life, creates 'children'. When the intimate encounter is performed with holiness, souls are created that are higher than angels. Spouses sometimes merit to draw down these souls into bodies, and there is a conception of a physical child. Other times, these souls remain bodiless, although they are real and they, too, have a tremendous impact on the family. As a result, a new soul-energy, a new light, rests in the home and between the spouses.

With a deeper comprehension of the spiritual nature of intimacy, it becomes abundantly clear that proper focus is vital. Besides the fact that attention and intention are crucial in any moment of life, it is even more true during intimacy. The state of mind we are in at the moment of intimacy will have a direct correlation to the type of 'souls' we create and draw down, whether physically or energetically. Loving and holy intimacy will create positive life force, manifesting itself in every aspect of the couple's married life.

Unfocused, ego-driven intimacy, or G-d forbid thinking about a different person during physical union (*Nedarim*, 20b) can create unfocused, unbalanced energy in one's life, marriage and home. And, even more devastatingly, if conception occurred at that moment, this will create children that will struggle with being focused and remaining on the mark, or even worse (*Rashi, Ran*, regarding Ben Sanuah, *ibid*). This is not meant to make anyone feel bad about their previous actions if they feel they were less than ideal, but only to make one more aware and sensitive to the powers and potentials of holy intimacy as they move forward in life. It is absolutely essential to point out that if one has made mistakes in the past, one should never despair of the power of *Teshuvah* / returning with strength to wholeness. In fact, when Teshuvah is initiated out of love, one's earlier errors may be transformed into hidden merits and revealed blessings. Mikvah immersion is a powerful tool in such a redemptive process.

Being Intimate Means Being Present

In the pages that follow, we will explore a variety of potential negative consequences that may result from mis-directed or distracted forms of intimacy, as expressed in Torah. It is important to note that although the following stories are focused on male characters, every character in Torah — whether the forefathers, foremothers, or even tribes — are both historical and archetypal, meaning that they represent psycho-spiritual qualities present within each and every one of us, regardless of gender. Therefore, no matter who we are, we can each find aspects of our souls and our experiences in the following stories.

From a certain perspective, one of the tragic figures in the Torah was the first born son of Yaakov, Reuven. It appears from the few stories the Torah tells about Reuven, that he always wanted to do the right thing, but was always a little off the mark with his actions. Although well-intentioned, his actions brought no positive result. Take, for instance, Reuven's attempt to save his brother Yoseph's life:

"And they (the brothers) saw him (Yoseph) from afar, and when he had not yet drawn near to them, they plotted against him to put him to death. So they said one to the other, 'Behold, that dreamer is coming. So now, let us kill him, and we will cast him into one of the pits, and we will say that a wild beast devoured him, and we will see what will become of his dreams.' But Reuven heard this plot, and he saved him from their hand(s), and he said, 'Let us not deal him a deadly blow.' And Reuven said to them, 'Do not shed blood! Cast him into this pit, which is in the desert, but do not lay a hand upon him.' (Reuven did so) in order to save him from their hand(s), (and) to return him to his father."

In the meantime, Reuven left his brothers and they sold him as a slave. "And Reuven returned to the pit, and behold, Yoseph was not in the pit, so he rent his garments" (*Bereishis*, 37:18-29). His true intention was to save his little brother, but, as discussed, his action bore no fruit.

In a quiet, enigmatic tale, the Torah tells us about another event, one that occurred shortly after the death of Rachel, the beloved wife of Yaakov. Yaakov had two primary wives, Leah (who was Reuven's mother) and Rachel (who was Yoseph's mother), and two handmaids, Zilpah, Leah's handmaid, and Bilhah, Rachel's handmaid. When Rachel passed away, this is what the Torah says, "And it came to pass... that Reuven went and lay with Bilhah, his father's concubine" (*Bereishis*, 35:22). What actually happened was that Reuven was trying to protect his mother's honor (*Shabbos*, 55b. Rashi, ad loc). When Rachel was alive, Yaakov kept his bed in Rachel's tent. When Rachel passed away, Yaakov moved his bed into the tent of Bilhah, Rachel's handmaid. When Reuven saw this, he said, "If my mother's sister was a rival to my mother, should my mother's sister's handmaid (now also) be a rival to my mother?"

Reuven understood that Yaakov loved Rachel, and all along wanted to marry her, even before he actually married his mother, Leah. So, if Yaakov wanted to place his bed in the tent of Rachel, it made sense. But, surely Rachel's handmaid held a lower position in the household than his mother

Leah, and so Reuven moved his father's bed from Bilhah's tent and placed it in the tent of his own mother, Leah.

His intentions were noble and honorable, yet, the Torah describes the event as a terrible sin, stating quizzically "that Reuven went and lay with Bilhah", although of course he did not actually lay with Bilhah (note, Rambam, *Hilchos Sotah*, 3:2. Although see *Kesef Mishnah*, ad loc). Why does the Torah then describe this event in the most misleading of ways? The Torah is trying to convey the message that Reuven's meddling in and moving his father's bed from one tent to the other without his consent, was upsetting to the delicate balance in his father's household. It was perhaps such an erosion of his father's authority in his own home, that caused Reuven to be considered as if he had (G-d forbid) committed incest with Bilhah.

The question emerges: What conditions created this imbalanced and misaligned personality? Perhaps, based on what we learned earlier, we can say that Reuven's nature is connected to his conception. After working for many years so that he could marry Rachel, Yaakov's father in law Lavan tricks him, and on the night of the wedding offers him his other daughter, Leah. That night Yaakov is intimate with Leah, all the while thinking that he is with Rachel. And the next morning, Yaakov is surprised: "And it came to pass in the morning, and behold she was Leah...(and he says) Why have you deceived me?" (*Bereishis*, 29:25). On that night,

Leah conceives Reuven (Bereishis, 49:3. *Rashi*, ad loc. *Yevamos*, 76a), specifically when Yaakov thinks he is being intimate with Rachel.

It is important to note that we are speaking relative to the level of the greatest of Tzadikim, the *Bechir haAvos* / the choicest of our forefathers, when we suggest that Reuven was conceived from an intimate encounter which was not focused. In general, a child born in such a situation is called a *Ben Temurah* / exchanged child, and that child may face certain spiritual challenges (*Nedarim*, 20b. Note, the language of the Rambam, where he brings an example of this, "(He) had the intent of having relations with his wife Rachel, and instead engaged in relations with his wife Leah" *Hilchos Isurei Biah*, 20:13). The mind of Yaakov was so occupied with Rachel that night, that the Zohar calls Reuven "Rachel's son" (*Zohar* 1, 17b. and 155a). Perhaps it is for this reason that Reuven suffers from relatively unfocused, off the mark actions. This trait was also shared with his brother Gad, as we will now explore.

There is something peculiar with the birth of Gad. When Yaakov is intimate with Gad's mother, Zilpah, the Torah simply says, *vaTeiled* / she 'bore' or birthed: "Leah's handmaid Zilpah bore Yaakov a son" (*Bereishis*, 30:9). With regard to all the other mothers, it says, *veTahar* / "she became pregnant." Why does the Torah omit the fact of pregnancy with regards to the birth of Gad? The Megaleh Amukos (Matos, Derush 4), reveals that Yaakov was intimate with Zilpah without *Shiduchim* / 'engagements', meaning courtship. Therefore, the Torah does not say, "And he was intimate with her, and she became pregnant" only that "Zilpah bore Yaakov a son."

Why did Yaakov not court Zilpah? Looking closely at the narrative, we can understand why Yaakov willingly lived with Bilhah, Rachel's maidservant, as Rachel was not yet able to have children at that point. By having children with Bilhah, it was as if he had children with Rachel. But then why did Yaakov need to have children with Zilpah, Leah's maidservant, as he had already had many children with Leah? The Torah says, "When Leah saw that she had stopped having children, she took her servant Zilpah and gave her to Yaakov as a wife" (*Bereishis*, 30:9). Leah desired as many children as possible, and she pushed Yaakov to be with Zilpah, even though he apparently had little interest. There is a fascinating Medrash to support this notion. Leah, perhaps knowing that Yaakov had little interest in Zilpah, dressed her that evening in her own garments, and when Yaakov was with her, he thought she was Leah, "as Zilpah was dressed as Leah" (Medrash, see *Torah Sheleimah*, Bereishis, 30:11) In other words, Yaakov was not thinking of Zilpah when he was intimate with her and conceived Gad, just as he was not thinking of Leah on the night Reuven was conceived.

As Reuven and Gad were conceived in unfocused intimacy, a type of unintentional action, these children and their entire tribes struggled with a penchant for unintentional actions and disastrous accidents. It is interesting to note that in proportion to the population, there were more 'cities of refuge' for people who killed by accident, in the east side of the Jordan River, the place where the tribes of Reuven and Gad settled, than in Eretz Yisrael proper. Why? Because there were more accidental killings among the tribes of Reuven and Gad than among the other tribes. (There were also more intentional killings: see *Makos*, 9b, *Tosefos*, "beGilad". *Gur Aryeh* (Maharal) Bamidbar, 35:14). Being prone to accidents, in general, suggests a type of haphazard, unfocused approach to living.

All of the above is merely meant to bring out this one important point: it is absolutely necessary to maintain one's presence and focus during intimacy, as the quality of a couple's attention on one another at this time when souls are brought down into the world, whether into bodies or not, is a determining factor in the nature of the soul or energy generated by their union. As we learned, the word Mikvah means 'gathering'. When immersing in the holy waters before intimacy, allow the Mikvah experience to gather your mind and heart into greater presence within yourself, in order to connect in higher purity with greater focus on your spouse.

Focused Water

Similarly, a deeper reason why waters that are *Sheuvim /* drawn do not create a Kosher Mikvah is because when spouses are intimate with each other without any distraction or ulterior motivations, it mirrors the perfectly focused and rectified unity between the upper, transcendent level of Yesod (masculine Divine attribute) with the lower, intimate level of Malchus (feminine Divine attribute). Thus, to facilitate and empower renewed intimacy, the woman must immerse in waters that embody this same unity.

There are always these two dimensions, masculine and feminine, within everything in Creation (*Baba Basra*, 74b). Rainwater descending from above to irrigate the earth below represents the masculine Heaven inseminating the feminine earth ("rain is the husband of the earth," *Ta'anis*, 6b), causing her to become pregnant with life and vegetation. Waters that are forcefully drawn or artificially coerced into a location other than the natural place of unity between Heaven and earth, embody a quality of misalignment and disunity, and thus it would not be appropriate for a woman to immerse in such waters before intimacy (*Rikanti*, Metzorah, 140a. *Yalkut Reuveini*, Metzorah, 33). A woman immersing in the Mikvah before intimacy, or for that matter a man (the Shaloh haKadosh writes that husbands should immerse in a Mikvah before intimacy, *Sha'ar HaOsyos*, Emek Beracha, Pei), should think about the unification of upper and lower waters, and how aligned intimacy and unity draws down new life and new souls into the world.

Allow the experience of Mikvah to help you let go of any distractions, be they personal, financial, mental, emotional or spiritual. Allow the Mikvah to help you consciously let go of all the Tumah in your life, both the literal Tumah of Nidah and also everything that Tumah represents. Release everything in your life that is closing you off from vitality, fluidity, flexibility and movement, anything at all that is closing you off from real intimacy with your spouse.

Maybe you are having a relatively difficult time in your relationship, maybe you are feeling upset or disappointed. Allow the Mikvah to wash all of this away, and help you begin anew, fresh and focused, able to join together in *Achdusa* / unity, *Chedvasa* / joy, and *Reusa* / desire.

Even worse than not being fully focused on each other would be to be intimate with one's spouse while angry and fighting (Chidah, see *Erech Apayim*, Siman 1, p. 55). Not only would one not be mentally present, in anger, one's whole self is not present. Anger clouds your vision to see outside of yourself and closes down your entire psyche. In anger, there is simply no room for another person. Sadly, children born from angry unions, whether they are physical or metaphysical beings, are negatively charged. A child conceived when spouses were fostering ill feelings towards each other is called a "child of quarrel" (*Nedarim*, 20b. Rambam, *Hilchos Isurei*

Biah, 21:12), and inherits spiritual struggle. Clearly, it is our responsibility as potential parents to not burden the souls generated from our intimate encounters with such avoidable issues.

The Mikvah is the perfect antidote for anger and other negative emotions. Let it be a place of letting go of all resentment and anger, a place of releasing the past and forging a better future. Allow the Mikvah to be a space of recognizing and recommitting to one's inherent unity with Hashem, with Torah and Mitzvos, with your higher self, your family, friends, community, and most importantly, with your spouse.

Following the separation of Nidah, a woman enters a state where she has new potential to create life, to play an essential role in generating Neshamos and even human bodies. The act of creating life in this way is the most Divine, *Ein Sof*, act there is, which stands in the closest resemblance to the Creator possible. To leave the subtly death-like energy of Tumah, and shift back into a place of life, a woman needs a radical transformation. Water is a transformative life-giving force. In its fluidity and constant movement, it is alive and capable even of reviving the dead, so to speak. Entering the waters of the Mikvah, a woman returns to the primordial womb of Creation, to her own source. Having reunified with the fountain of all life, she emerges ready to be a source of life herself.

The post-Nidah immersion should be used to contemplate reconnecting tangibly with the Source of All Life and Giving, opening oneself again to engaging with purposeful life and focused intimacy, free of all negativity, judgment and distraction. It is an opportunity to let go of everything standing in the way of pure, loving presence and *Shalom Bayis* / harmony and peace in the home. This is the time to connect to the 'living waters', as well as the 'lower waters', which draw new life down from above, possibly even in the form of luminous, healthy children.

CHAPTER 8

~~~

Mikvah Erev Shabbos

EVERYTHING THAT EXISTS IN SPACE ALSO EXISTS IN TIME, AND EVERYTHING THAT EXISTS IN TIME ALSO EXISTS IN SPACE. Just as there is a *Beis ha-Mikdash* / Holy Temple that belongs to the realm of space, there is a Beis haMikdash within the realm of time, and that is Shabbos. On Shabbos, we enter the Beis haMikdash of time.

In the spatial Beis haMikdash, the *Cohen* / Priest who served there needed a special means of transitioning from the outside, mundane world, into that inner, sacred space. He was required to wash his hands and feet with water, to immerse himself in a Mikvah (*Yumah*, 30a), and to don special garments (without the clothes, his status was not of a 'full Cohen', *Zevachim*, 17b). The same means allow us to transition into the temporal Temple, Shabbos. We, too, need to wash ourselves, at least our hands and feet (*Shabbos*, 25b. Shulchan Aruch, *Orach Chayim*, 260:1), and for extra measure, immerse ourselves in a Mikvah, and put on special garments for Shabbos (*Shabbos*, 113a).

Transitions

To be fully present and engaged with any situation that arises, we need a liminal or transitional state, wherein we can move gradually and consciously from one reality into another. For example, say you are finishing up a hard day's work, where you were stressed out and overwhelmed with financial pressure, and now you need to go to your best friend's wedding; you cannot rush straight from work to the wedding. If you do so, you might arrive physically, but you will not be truly present; your mind and heart will still be at work. You will be schlepping all your stress into a situation that is supposed to be joyous. What is required is an in-between state, a place or time to move out of your work consciousness and enter into wedding consciousness. Certain physical activities can help you do this, such as taking a shower and putting on different clothes, for example.

With regard to the holy day of Shabbos, we need to leave the work-week behind in order to transition into a deeper and higher, more spiritual Shabbos state of being. We need a proper liminal space and time where we can literally and figuratively remove the 'garments' of the week, and elevate ourselves into the Holy Sanctuary of Shabbos.

Techniques of transition are particularly essential when it comes to Shabbos, as Shabbos starts in the midst of a weekday, so to speak. If we would go to sleep on a weekday and wake up in the morning to the beginning of Shabbos, then the sleep itself would serve as the liminal experience of transition, providing a veritable passageway between worlds, so to speak. We would simply go to sleep and wake up in a different state of consciousness. However, this is not how Torah time works. Days begin at night, not in the morning. Therefore, Shabbos starts late Friday afternoon, effectively in the middle of the day. In more northern locations Shabbos can begin as early as 3pm, and even earlier in certain places. Due to this dynamic, it is absolutely essential to learn how to transition from one state into another while we are still awake, for Shabbos arrives amid the pressures of the weekday.

What is more striking is that, if Shabbos or candle lighting time is at 3:34pm, at 3:33 and 59 seconds we are still technically in the weekday, and only one second later, we are submerged in the completely different atmosphere of Shabbos. There is no in-between time, therefore we must create one ourselves; we thus need to actively engage and harness transitional practices, to help us move with our whole being into the temporal Temple of Shabbos. This is the gift of the Mikvah.

Water, as explored earlier, is the perfect medium for effecting transition, as it has no *Tzurah* / form, and when we enter water, we are *Poshet Tzurah* / removing and releasing any attachments to the old Tzurah. While immersed in water, we are able to experience ourselves without form. As we penetrate the roof of the water, emerge from the Mikvah and start getting dressed, we are *Lovesh Tzurah* / garbing ourselves in a new Tzurah, the sanctified vessels of Shabbos. When we entered the building of the Mikvah, we were completely enmeshed in our old Tzurah and weekday garments, and now as we leave, we have donned the new Tzurah and garments of Shabbos.

Even without fully immersing in the Mikvah, contact with water can facilitate transition. This is because water, in any form, cleanses and resets our energetic coordinates. For instance, as a People just freed from Egypt, Klal Yisrael needed to pass through a body of water to fully transition out of their identity as slaves, into a new identity of free people with limitless potential. After decades of oppression and trauma, Klal Yisrael suddenly emerged from the yoke of Egypt and traveled through the *Keriyas Yam Suf* / the Splitting of the Sea. It was only after passing through the Sea that the ex-slaves were truly free, and that Egypt, and everything it represented, no longer threatened or impinged upon their freedom. This is one reason for the practical and Halachic requirement to bathe or shower on Erev Shabbos. Of course a Mikvah is the optimal vessel of transformation, but we learn countless times in the Torah that the nature of water itself is to transform and revivify. Therefore, even if we do not observe the custom of immersing in a Mikvah before Shabbos, we are all required to bathe ourselves with water in some capacity.

It is important to note that bathing or showering before Shabbos is considered a separate issue from Mikvah, and should be done even if one goes to the Mikvah. Again, bathing is a requirement, whereas pre-Shabbos immersion in a Mikvah is a custom or voluntary spiritual practice. However, it is also important to stress that while all contact with water is potentially transformational, the release of our past self achieved by Mikvah immersion affords us the most effective and smoothest transition into a Shabbos state of being.

Water and the Nature of Shabbos

Besides being the perfect medium of transition into Shabbos, for all the reasons explored above, water is also intricately connected to the concept of Shabbos itself.

Fire and water are the two dominant elements of Creation, representing the polar opposites of the weekly dynamic: fire is the quality of the weekday, and water is the quality of Shabbos.

Fire suggests creation, productivity and progress. Fire refines and 'completes' objects, such as in cooking and making them edible. The beginning of human civilization is Adam's discovery of fire, which gave rise to the technologies of processing and preserving foods, melding and fashioning tools, illuminating the dark and warming the cold.

Human beings did not 'steal fire from Heaven', as many people believed in the past. Quite the opposite, Hashem lovingly gave us the gift of fire. Fire allows us to 'work'— to participate in Creation, making use of the world around us and manipulating its forces for our benefit, and the benefit of all creatures. All of this and more is included in the energy and paradigm of the weekdays, the Six Days of Creation.

On the Seventh Day, Shabbos, we are not allowed to continue any of this *Melachah* / work. There are 39 *Avos* / 'parent' or main forms of work that are prohibited to engage, and many more *Toldos* / 'offspring' of these prohibitions. Yet, the Torah singles out the act of lighting fire as the archetypal prohibition on Shabbos: (*Shabbos*, 70a): "Do not light a fire in all your dwellings on the Shabbos day" (*Shemos*, 35:3. The Torah also mentions not plowing or harvesting, *Shemos*, 34:21). This is because using fire is the most pronounced form of Melachah, and in a way it is the root of all human creative skill and ingenuity.

Shabbos, like water, is the very antithesis to fire. Water unifies multiplicity into a greater whole. Similarly, Shabbos brings together the disparate energies of the week, providing them with a unified purpose and direction.

Water is an undifferentiated, seamless body. Every drop in the ocean is one with the entire ocean. As explored earlier, water is generally called *Mayim*, plural, whereas the 'correct' word for water should be *Mai*, in the singular. So why is water called *Mayim*? A body of water is where individual drops of water come together as one unit. Even the smallest droplet on the head of a pin contains trillions of water molecules. Water is 'a many that is one' (*Ideres Eliyahu*, Bereishis, 1:9).

Scientifically speaking, although water seems like a seamless whole, in fact, each molecule of water contains polar opposite compounds, one oxygen and two hydrogen atoms (thus water is known as H2O), which are connected through a particular bonding agent. As these compounds are attracted and pulled towards each other, all these individual molecules of water form a cohesive whole. In other words, water is in fact a polarity, a duality, a multiplicity that is formed into a cohesive and unified whole. Water is unity, and the nature of water is to unify.

Water brings objects closer to each other, connecting and fusing them. Fire splinters things apart, disconnects, and disperses them. When fire does connect and join, such as in welding together pieces of metal, it can only do this when it renders solid objects soft and water-like. The liquidizing of the metal, plastic or wax reveals the element of 'water' within the fire. This, too, shows that water is the prime unifying agent, as water exists subtly even within the other elements. (Similarly, when water dissolves and breaks things apart, it is showing its ability to unify with the essence of fire.)

Fire is *Gevurah* / strength, boundaries, resistance, individuation. This characterizes the energy of the week. Water is *Chesed* / kindness, the quality of gathering and giving, drawing closer, connecting and unifying. This is exactly the power of Shabbos.

During the week we are, so to speak, standing outside of nature and manipulating it for our ends. Sometimes we find ourselves at odds with nature, and maybe even at war with it. There can often seem to be an existential separation and friction between us and the natural forces around us. This is the weekday paradigm, the quality of fire. On Shabbos, we are in the world like fish in water, so to speak. There is no more resistance, friction or fracture between us and the world around us. On Shabbos, there is the holistic unity and flow of the inner spirit of water.

On a simplistic level, this unity is reflected in the fact that on Shabbos, we spend more time becoming closer with our families and communities. More inwardly, it is a time to become closer to our deeper selves, more unified with our Neshamah and with Hashem. Shabbos is, on the most fundamental level, "a day of the soul".

Shabbos is spelled Shin/300, Beis/2, Tav/400, totalling 702. In *Mispar Katan* / small numeric value, this can be reduced to the numerals 7 and 2. The number 72 is the value of the word *Chesed* / kindness, alluding to its primary resident energy and further connecting it to water. Shabbos, like water, is kind, welcoming, harmonious and nurturing. Therefore, to transition out of the competition and distance of the weekday paradigm of 'fire', and into the closeness and generosity of the Shabbos paradigm of 'water', we need immerse ourselves in the waters of the Mikvah.

Leaving the Concealments of Elokim and Entering 'a Day to Hashem'

Shabbos is called a *Yom laHashem* / a day to Hashem (*Devarim*, 5:13), whereas the weekdays, and the natural world, are more connected to the Name Elokim. Elokim is the Divine aspect that is immanent and revealed within the workings of nature (Elokim and *haTeva* / nature have the same numeric value, 86), the Name Hashem, on the other hand, represents the Divine dimension of Infinity and Transcendence of nature. Elokim is strict judgment, expressed in the 'laws of nature'. Hashem is boundless mercy, expressed in the possibility for Teshuvah.

Mikvah is numerically 151 (Mem/40 + Kuf/100 + Vav/6 + Hei/5 = 151), and this is the same value of two Divine Names that are specifically connected to the restrictive, concealing quality of *Gevurah* / strength: the Name Elokim (86) and the Name Ado-noi (65) (86 + 65 = 151). By immersing in a Mikvah, we are nullifying all the concealments and restrictions of the past work-week and opening ourselves up to receive the unconstricted Divine Chesed of the Infinite One.

Mayim is spelled Mem (40), Yud (10), Mem (40), the sum of which is 90. When the letter Yud is extended it becomes a Vav, and in that case, in place of Mayim (Mem-Yud-Mem) there is *Mum* (Mem/4, Vav/6, Mem/40). *Mum* means 'defect' or imperfection, and has a sum of 86, the same as the Name *Elokim*, and as the word *haTeva* / nature.

As the work-week is coming to a close, we leave the natural world of Elokim, the world of process and imperfection (meaning the concealment of actual perfection), and seek to enter Shabbos, the Yom laHashem, a foretaste of *Olam haBa* / the future world of revealed perfection. Thus, we immerse ourselves in the Mikvah and transform ourselves and the world around us, from a world of *Mum* to a world of *Mayim*, unity and Chesed.

The Zohar talks about the four possible ways to 'fill' the letters of the Name of Hashem (Yud-Hei-Vav-Hei). For example, the letter Hei can be spelled Hei/5, Yud/10, or it can be spelled Hei/5, Aleph /1, yielding different sums; the same holds true for all four letters of the Divine Name. Therefore, depending on how the four letters Yud-Hei-Vav-Hei are spelled out, the full numeric value of the Name of Hashem can be either 72, 63, 45, or 52.*

---

* **Yud**/10, Vav/6, Dalet/4=20. Hei/5, **Yud**/10=15. Vav/6, **Yud**/10, Vav/6= 22. Hei/5, **Yud**/10=15. 20+15+22+15=72 (Av).

Yud/10, Vav/6, Dalet/4=20. Hei/5, **Yud**/10=15. Vav/6, *Aleph*/1, Vav/6=13. Hei/5, **Yud**/10=15. 20+15+13+15= 63 (Sag).

Yud/10, Vav/6, Dalet/4=20. Hei/5, *Aleph*/1= 6. Vav/6, *Aleph*/1, Vav/6= 13. Hei/5, *Aleph*/1=6. 20+6+13+6= 45 (Mah).

Yud/10, Vav/6, Dalet/4=20. Hei/5, *Hei*/5= 10. Vav/6, Vav/6=12. Hei/5, *Hei*/5=10. 20+10+12+10=52 (Ban)

Throughout all of these four possible spellings, there are nine letter Yuds. Yud is numerically 10, and 10 times 9 equals 90 — which again is the value of the word *Mayim*. When a person is entering into Mayim, they are thus entering into the Name of Hashem. This is a very important *Kavanah* / intention (*Pri Eitz Chayim*, Sha'ar haShabbos, 1, Sod haTevilah. Shaloh, *Maseches Shabbos*, 88. *Sha'ar haOsyos*, Kedushah, 8. *Kanfei Yonah*, Sod haTevilah), and one that can help you smoothly transition from the days that are dominated by nature and the body, into the "Day of the Soul", as the Zohar calls Shabbos (*Zohar* 2, 205b. 3, 174a).

In order to enter the 'Day of Hashem', we should first enter the 'Name of Hashem'. When surrounded by the 'waters of Hashem', we can release the constrictions of the Name Elokim, and shed the fiery energy of the week, with all its stressful ambition and drive for productivity. The Gevurah of the weekdays then gives way to the Chesed of Shabbos, and we can more easily enter its expansive, peaceful, gentle, water-like reality.

Entering Olam haBa

Water is the primordial state of Creation. As explored earlier, there was a time when the earth was completely "covered with water", and yet the Torah does not explicitly describe the creation of water. It is something out of the ordinary, seemingly even outside of this world. Creatures that live in the water also seem to be other-worldly or primordially ancient. Early Mekubalim write that fish originate from an earlier *Shemitah* / 'cycle of Creation' (*Sefer haKana*, "Mi Mutar baAchilos Basar". *Yalkut Reuveini*, Bereishis, 248-249). That earlier Shemitah is known as the cycle of Chesed, a water-like era, whereas our current cycle is one of Gevurah, *Din* / constriction and definitions. (*Sefer haTemunah*, Hakdamah, Temunah 3. *Yalkut Reuveini*, Bereishis, 20).

Water has a closer affinity with the world of spirit than the world of matter. We feel a sense of purity, vitality, mystery and transcendence near water. We are taught, "Every place where the Divine presence rests, there you will find water" (*Megaleh Amukos*, Terumah, 18:8). According to many opinions (based on the *Mechilta*, Shemos, 12:1. *Tanchumah*, Bo, 5. *Sifri*, Shoftim, 32), once Eretz Yisrael was chosen as the Sacred Land, prophecy generally occurs only in Eretz Yisrael (*Umunos v'De'os*, Ma'amar 3:5. *Kuzari*, 2:14. *Ramban*, Devarim, 18:15. *Teshuvas haRashba*, 548. *Rashi*, Moed Katan, 25a). When, however, under certain conditions, prophecy occurs outside of Eretz Yisrael, it only occurs in a place near water (*Mechilta*, ibid. See *Zohar* 1, 222b. *Zohar* 2, 82b). Water connects the prophet to a higher, purer world, placing him in closer proximity to the primordial state of Creation and to the redeemed world of the future.

Our Sages tell us that *Olam haZeh* / this world is like dry land, and *Olam haBa* / the World to Come is like the sea

(*Koheles Rabbah*, 1:9). Our relationship to this physical world is based on a perception of density and separation. Olam haBa is likened to water, flowing and unified. As water represents the primordial and pure world of infinite potential and possibility, it evokes the total unity between ourselves and the world around us.

Indeed, this is what we should have in mind when we enter a Mikvah, especially before or on Shabbos. We are entering into the space of World to Come, and connecting with something much deeper than the immediacy and tangibility of Olam haZeh. "A person should have in mind when he enters into a Mikvah that he is entering into the Higher Waters, which is the secret of Olam haBa" (*Reishis Chochmah*, Sha'ar haAhavah, 11). When we enter the Mikvah we are entering a different realm, a higher reality.

Shabbos, too, is like Olam haBa (*Berachos*, 57b. *Mechilta*, Shemos, 31:13). What better means to enter Olam haBa, than to immerse in the waters of Olam haBa.

Bath and Mikvah

As mentioned earlier in this chapter, there is a Mitzvah to perform *Rechitzah* / washing before Shabbos, to actually bathe or take a shower, and specifically in hot water. Rechitzah and Mikvah represent two separate ideas, cleansing and purifying.

On Erev Shabbos, in honor of Shabbos, Rabbi Yehudah would wash himself with hot water, particularly his hands, face and feet (*Shabbos*, 25b). We, too, should bathe or shower our entire body and also our hair (*Shabbos*, 31a), and the Halacha is to do so specifically with hot water (*Shulchan Aruch*, Orach Chaim, Siman 260:1. *Gra* ad loc). The simple reason for this washing is for cleanliness, to prepare and groom the body in order to honor Shabbos.

According to most rulings, Rechitzah should certainly not be done with cold water (*Biur Halacha*, 260:1), and even lukewarm water is not sufficient (*Noda b'Yehudah*, 2:24). The reason is twofold: hot water both cleanses better and simultaneously releases tension. Shabbos is a time of rest and ease, characterized by an absence of struggle and strife; taking a hot bath or shower literally softens the body and releases built up tension. Tension can be appropriate and even productive during the work-week, yet on Shabbos, we need to slip into a world and consciousness of harmony and peace. Therefore, bathing the body in hot water before Shabbos physically releases us and inwardly untangles us from the tensions of the work-week.

On a more spiritual level, we are washing our bodies from the *Tumah* / impurities, the blockages, the concealments and obstructions of connection and flow. In this way we are readied to assume an even higher form of Teharah, purity and Kedushah through the Mikvah. In the words of the holy Zohar, "As Shabbos is about to approach, the holy people must wash their bodies of the mark of the profane week. For what reason? Because during the week another spirit (from the 'Other Side') comes forth and rests upon the people. So, when people want to move away from this (negative) spirit and to ascend to a higher spirit, a holy spirit, they must bathe, so that the supernal holy spirit may rest on them" (*Zohar* 2, 204a).

Hot water, teaches the Arizal (Rabbi Yitzchak Luria, 1534-1572, the preeminent master of the deeper teachings of the Torah), pushes aside and repels all the spiritual dirt, Kelipah, concealment and negativity, so that Kelipah cannot be nourished by Shabbos (*Sha'ar haKavanos*). Just as Neshamos are cleansed in *Nahar Dinor* / the supernal River of Fire, before Shabbos, we need to wash our bodies in a flow of hot water (*Tikunei Zohar*, Hakdamah, 4) to purge and eliminate the accumulated energies of the past week. Inwardly, Kelipah is experienced as our worries, doubts and hurts, our anger, depression and small-mindedness, our negative attachments, and lack of *Emunah* / faith and *Bitachon* / trust. And so, we harness the power of *Shalheves* / a lit torch (the torch of Yud and Hei), and 'burn' away all these Kelipos (*Sha'ar haKavanos*, from *Zohar* 2, Vayakhel, 203a) by washing ourselves with hot water, which is considered like going into the purifying *Nahar Dinor* / River of Fire (Chidah, *Devash lePhi*, Reish, 10).

The Arizal also speaks specifically about the three body parts, the hands, face and feet, that Rabbi Yehudah washed, and explains that these are the three places where 'impurity' accumulates. Therefore, washing them before Shabbos removes these impurities. In fact, the Arizal also teaches that there is an order to how the body is to be washed; first the head and face, then the right hand, the left hand, the right leg, and finally the left leg.

More recently, the Ben Ish Chai, Rabbi Yosef Chayim (1832-1909) of Baghdad, spoke about washing the furthest tips of the body, the hands and toes, and when doing so to have in mind to release all Kelipah (*Ben Ish Chai*, Lech Lecha 15). When we physically release dirt, sweat, oils and dead skin cells, we are physiologically releasing mental and emotional tension, psychologically releasing negative thoughts and emotions, and spiritually releasing ourselves from the hold of the Kelipos. At the same time we are opening ourselves up, physically, psychologically and spiritually to receive the Kedushah of Shabbos.

Physical dirt and fungus collect especially at the 'tips' of the body, the fingernails and toenails. The physical mirrors the spiritual. For this reason, the Zohar tells us that spiritual Kelipah also gathers on or under the fingernails and toenails, and thus they need to be both cleaned and trimmed on Erev Shabbos. Halacha also guides us to cut our nails on Erev Shabbos (*Shulchan Aruch*, Orach Chayim, 260:1. Nails are

Tumah, *Tola'as Yaakov*, p. 23. Nails are Kelipah, *Zohar* 2, 208b. Radbaz, *Metzudas Dovid*, 38). Cutting the nails is akin to cutting away the hard, sharp or aggressive nature of the work-week.

In this respect, it appears from the writings of the Arizal that he would cut his nails after midday on Friday, at some point after immersing in the Mikvah (although, for women's Mikvah cutting the nails is done before the immersion. *Shach*, Yoreh De'ah, 198:25). The disciples of the Rebbe Maharash, Rabbi Shmuel of Chabad, asked him when he would cut his nails on Erev Shabbos. He said that he does so after the bath and Mikvah, 'because then his nails are soft.' This is, of course, a literal fact, but it also alludes to something deeper: when you are softened, and your tensions are diminished, it is easier to get rid of all your Kelipah and anything holding you back, whether negativities or just trivialities.

In all cases, after a thorough bath or shower, one is ready to immerse in the Mikvah (Shaloh, *Meseches Shabbos*, 9. The Chidah, *Birchei Yoseph*, 260:3. From other sources it seems clear that one should shower *after* the Mikvah, sometime later during the day: *Derushei Seder Shabbos*, Derush 1, Inyan Kabbalas Shabbos. See also, *Chemdas haYamim*, Shabbos Kodesh, 3. *Yesod Shoresh haAvodah*, Sha'ar 8, Sha'ar Elyon, 1. On the other hand, there are other issues with showering right after the Mikvah, especially for Ashkenazim: see *Rama*, Yoreh De'ah, 201:75, in the name of the Mordechai and Rashbam. Sha'ch, ad loc, 151). Whereas the shower or bath was taken specifically in heated water, as the 'fire' of the water burns away all the spiritual and physical dirt, the Mikvah is ideally a little cooler so that it refreshes and wakes one up.

The custom of the Arizal was not to dry himself when he came out of the Mikvah on Erev Shabbos. In other words, he would put on his dry clothes over the waters on his body. Many people, today, may find this unsettling, uncomfortable and even distracting, and thus counterproductive.

Perhaps hundreds of years ago and in warm climates, refraining from drying oneself after the Mikvah may have been a real option. Additionally, the clothes that were worn in non-European and non-Westernized countries, such as Israel and Egypt where the Arizal lived, were very loose fitting and flowing, more like robes or cloaks, and putting these on over a wet body was not so uncomfortable. Our modern clothes are comparatively tight-fitting, making moisture uncomfortable or irritating. In cold weather, it is also common sense to avoid going outdoors while still wet. Furthermore, our Sages say that putting on shoes when the feet are wet is dangerous, and can damage one's eyesight (*Pesachim*, 111b). This is not merely words of *Agadah* / deeper spiritual narrative, rather it is actually mentioned in practical Halacha (*Shulchan Aruch haRav*, Hilchos Shmiras Guf vNefesh, 9). Therefore, one should dry their feet very well before getting dressed, and very importantly also, their face (*Shabbos*, 113b. *Shulchan Aruch*, Orach Chayim, 4:20).

However, if you did want to connect with the custom of the Arizal, you could, as some sources have suggested, dry your entire body except for one small area (*Ben Ish Chai*, Lech Lecha, 17:6. The Rebbe, *Toras Menachem*, 5743 vol 1, p. 386; many have suggested the knee), and allow the waters of the Mikvah on that area to be absorbed into your body.

Two Stages

The transition into Shabbos thus has two stages: cleansing oneself and then acquiring purity, Rechitzah and then Mikvah. First, there is an elimination of the negative, and then, an assuming of the positive. First, we need to leave the energy of the weekday and *Olam haZeh* / this world, and then, we can enter the Mikvah and assume the holiness, purity and aliveness of the world of *Olam haBa* / the World to Come and of Shabbos.

When Rav Hamnuna, the mystic sage in the Zohar, would ascend from the river in which he had immersed, he would lift up his eyes and observe the angels or energetic qualities of the weekday ascending on high, and the angels or energies of Shabbos descending in this world (*Zohar* 2, 136b). Not everyone is prepared for or privy to such insight and vision, but that does not mean it is not there to be seen. In truth, this is actually what happens when anyone immerses, and Rav Hamnuna was simply able to observe it visually.

When we enter a Mikvah on Erev Shabbos, we are beginning to receive the 'extra soul' of Shabbos. It is this 'extra soul', this extra level of spiritual awareness, which allows us to experience a deeper vision of reality (*Reishis Chochmah*, Sha'ar Kedushah, 8).

The removal of the garments of the weekday and the deep cleansing of the body represent the ascent of the 'angels' of the weekday. Tevilah is both the total *Bitul* / nullification of the entire weekday paradigm, as well as the receiving of the descending blessings of Shabbos — this is the *Neshamah Y'seirah* / additional level of soul that opens us to experience a glimmer of the World to Come.

Bitul, the state of Ayin, can give us the experience of feeling free from the Yesh of this world — free from financial responsibilities, free from worry, doubt, anger, jealousy and lustful attachments. The Bitul that we experience in the Mikvah is a foretaste of the state that we will function in during the entire Shabbos.

Shabbos is a Mikvah of Time

Every *Mitzvah* / Divine command exists within the realm of *Olam* / space, *Shanah* / time, and *Nefesh* / soul or consciousness. The Mikvah that we enter before Shabbos is a Mikvah in space, and through that portal of space we enter a Mikvah in time, the holy, transcendental day of Shabbos.

By 'immersing' in Shabbos we immerse ourselves in the World to Come. On Shabbos, we have taken leave of Olam haZeh, the world of Yesh. This is similar to when we are underwater and can no longer breathe or 'exist' as an individual, but only exist within a state of transcendence. When we step into the 'temporal Mikvah' of Shabbos, we have released ourselves from the constant hustle and grind of the work-week, letting go of our productive engagement in bettering the world, and by extension, our worry, anxiety and tension. We then immerse fully in the atmosphere of Shabbos, and operate in a state of Bitul for 25 or 26 hours. (26 is significant as it is the numeric value of the Four Letter Name of Hashem.) During this entire time, we are in the World to Come, in the world of Ayin, of Transcendence, of the Soul — the World of Hashem.

The six days correspond to Yesh, and Shabbos corresponds to Ayin.

For six days a week we labor in a paradigm of *Elokim*, the perspective of Yesh, of form. We express our 'form' by manipulating the world to further our goals — from instinctual physical 'needs' to financial or even spiritual goals. On Shabbos, we rest from all goals. We cease from expressing our own 'form' in the world, and are content to just be. On Shabbos, we enter the formlessness of Ayin, the existential, experiential emptiness of all 'things' and all 'doing'.

Without a pause, without Shabbos, we would toil endlessly in the world of Yesh, accumulating more and more 'form' until it would all become oppressive. We would ultimately end up so enslaved to our goals and possessions that we would be crushed by their burden. By leaving all of that behind and immersing in an Ayin state throughout the time of Shabbos, we become light, free and effortlessly conscious of our soul, which is in fact the Ayin, Transcendence within us, that which is "a part of Hashem, literally".

For all the reasons explored above, Mikvah is the perfect medium to get us into the head-space and heart-space of Ayin; it is the spatial embodiment of Ayin, freedom from the weight of form. The Mikvah, like the Beis haMikdash, is therefore a representation of Olam haBa in 'space'. When we immerse in the Mikvah's living waters before Shabbos, we also enter into the 'time' of Olam haBa, the 'Day to Hashem', as well as the 'consciousness' of Olam haBa, the *Neshamah Y'seirah* / heightened identification as an infinite soul. Mikvah thus provides one with the opportunity to complete the structure of space, time and soul in relation to Shabbos.

～～

CHAPTER 9

~~~~

Mikvah Everyday

EVERY MORNING, UPON AWAKENING, WE RIT-
UALLY WASH OUR HANDS. We fill a washing cup
with water (ideally prior to sleep), place it near our
bed with a basin, and upon waking we pour it over each
hand, alternating so that each hand is washed three times.

There are many reasons offered for this washing (*Rosh*, Berachos, 9:23. Rambam, *Hilchos Tefilah*, 4:1. See *Pri Megadim*, Orach
Chayim, 4:1). One is that during sleep, our hands may have
involuntarily touched an unclean place of the body. Another is that, washing our hands serves as a preparation for
the holy act of prayer, similar to the *Cohanim* / Priests who
would wash their hands prior to performing their tasks in
the *Beis haMikdash* / Holy Temple. When we pray each day,
we are like a Cohen, and even like the Cohen Gadol / High
Priest, serving in the Temple (*Teshuvas haRashba*, 1:191).

The Zohar explains (*Zohar* 1, 184b. see also; *Shabbos*, 109a and the
Pri Megadim, ibid) that when a person is asleep, a spirit of Tumah rests upon their entire body, and when they awaken,
this spirit departs from the body, remaining only upon the
hands. Pouring water over the hands releases this last rem-
nant of Tumah from the body (*Shulchan Aruch haRav*, 4:4). In
the morning, following the Tumah of the night, we become
a *Beriyah Chadashah* / new creation, and we wash our hands
to symbolically initiate our new life (Rashba, *ibid*).

Water connects us to Teharah, to life, movement and newness, and takes us away from all Tumah, death, stagnancy and staleness. But why does sleep subject us to Tumah?

Sleep is "one-sixtieth of death" (*Berachos*, 57b). When a person is asleep, they are not being creative or productive in an ordinary sense. The body, and to some extent the mind, is dormant and inactive. Of course, sleep is healing, healthy and necessary. It's temporary cessation, like Shabbos, is what allows creativity to take place in the first place. Ideas absorbed while awake become more deeply ingrained in one's consciousness while asleep. Yet, on an observable level, when a person is asleep, they are in a death-like state in which they are not visibly acting and engaging with the world around them.

As is now abundantly clear, any lack of vitality or movement is the opposite of Teharah and holiness. As the body lies asleep, though it is in the process of recharging, it is in a state of Tumah. Thus we wash our hands with water, the great 'agent of transformation', to transform our dormancy and rigidity into wakefulness, freshness, purity, possibility and *Chayus* / life. These waters also reconnect us to the world of Unity and Olam haBa.

To enter the Beis haMikdash, the Cohen would employ 'water' to transition from the 'mundane' space outside the Temple, the space connected to the world of (possible) Tumah, into the sacred, dynamic space where nothing could become old or stale (*Chagigah*, 26b), a world of total presence, the absence of 'sleep' (Bereishis, 28:16, *Rashi*). The same is true within the dimension of time. In order to move from the quality of night and the temporary 'death' and stillness of sleep into the fresh, new day of life and movement, we also need contact with water. When we begin our morning this way, we instill a sense of sacredness in our efforts to engage with the world; we demonstrate that the qualities of Kedushah and Teharah, transcendence and purity, are the foundation upon which all our ensuing actions and efforts will unfold.

The letter of the law directs us to this practice of handwashing upon awakening. Beyond the letter of the law, however, and a custom of those who are more mystically inclined and spiritually sensitive, is to also fully immerse their entire bodies in a Mikvah every morning. This, too, is in the image of the Cohen, who would wash his hands and feet before entering the Beis haMikdash, and then also immerse himself completely in a Mikvah (*Yumah*, 30a). He would then don special garments appropriate to his service to the Creator. Accordingly, we may also wash our hands, then fully immerse, and finally don garments for our service of Tefilah and interaction with the world. (Our clothing, our interface with the world, is part of the new Yesh that we assume after our morning immersion. Like the Cohen, it helps facilitate our particular *Avodah* / spiritual work and spiritual calling.)

Full immersion empowers us to remain invigorated, re-freshed, fluid, and hopeful throughout the entire day, and keeps any Tumah and Kelipah from attaching itself to us, pulling us down, or making us feel weak or gloomy. Such is the power of the holy waters of the Mikvah. Following sleep, we are between night (death, Tumah) and day (life, Teharah). This is a powerful time to steer the entire day toward Kedushah and Teharah. Thus on any day, as on Erev Shabbos, we may choose to keep a small area of the body wet from the waters of the Mikvah, allowing the body to absorb their blessings (*Osrei leGefen,* 16, p. 357).

When we awake from our slumber and are about to venture out into the world, immersing fully in the transformative waters of the Mikvah makes the transition easier. However, Mikvah not only affects our entrance into the new day, but our entire day will be more filled with Teharah, connec-tivity and light, on account of our immersion. As the very foundation of our day is established within the Mikvah, the rest of the day will be one long unfolding of the power of Mikvah.

~~~

CHAPTER 10

~~~

Mikvah as a Tikkun for Anger & Other Negative States

THE MIKVAH EMPOWERS US TO CHANGE AND GROW IN A DIRECTION OF HOLINESS AND HEIGHTENED CONSCIOUSNESS. It empowers us to be who we really are, and to serve and engage the world in the ways we are meant to.

For these reasons, some people are obligated, according to Torah law, to immerse in a Mikvah. A convert immerses once in their lifetime, a woman perhaps once a month. Others are encouraged, according to rabbinic law and custom, to immerse at different intervals. All may immerse once a year on Erev Yom Kippur, some men immerse after being intimate with their spouses; and those who follow deeper practices immerse at least once a week, on Erev Shabbos, or every morning after a night of sleep, a subtle encounter with death, as explored.

In addition, since Mikvah purifies and un-binds us from all forms of Tumah, some who are more spiritually inclined and sensitive might immerse at any time, even within a single day, such as during certain stages of Shabbos. They might also immerse any time they feel spiritually pulled down, heavy or lethargic. In other words, whenever any type of Tumah sets in, one may counter that existential inertia by immersing in a Mikvah.

Every negative emotion creates a form of Tumah, a death of sorts. For example, when a person insults or embarrasses another, they 'kill' them, so-to-speak: "He who publicly shames his neighbor is as if he shed blood" (*Baba Metziya*, 58b). When a person robs another, even of a few cents, it is as if he "stole their soul" (*Baba Metziya*, 112a), another subtle form of death. This is essentially the case with every negative trait or act. Besides the *Issur* / prohibition on many such acts, there is also a death-like Tumah that inhabits a person who has committed one of them. In fact, Isur is also called Tumah (*Sotah*, 9b. *Chulin*, 140a. *Avodah Zarah*, 36a. See also *Beis haOtzer* [Engel], Aleph, 129).

Therefore, in addition to asking for forgiveness from the other who was embarrassed, or returning the money that was stolen and asking forgiveness, immersion in a Mikvah is most beneficial in untangling oneself from the Tumah produced by these misdeeds (Shaloh, *Sha'ar haOsyos*, Teharah, 11).

Anger & the Mikvah

More destructive than nearly all other negative temperaments, behaviors, words, or thoughts is anger and its accompanying Tumah. A person who has flared up in anger, even subtly, should make a Tikkun for this and undo the subsequent inner damage by immersing in a Mikvah.

Ka'as / anger, in numeric value, equals 150 (Chaf/20 + Ayin/70 + Samach/60 = 150), and adding 1 for the word itself, equals 151.[*]

---

[*] The "word" is also counted in this numeric value, writes the Shaloh,

Similarly, the usual Torah word for 'wrathful' is *Kanah*, which in numeric value is also 151 (Kuf/100 + Nun/50 + Aleph/1=151). *Mikvah* as well is numerically 151 (Mem/40 + Kuf/100 + Vav/6 + Hei/5=151). This suggests an intrinsic connection between immersion in the Mikvah and overcoming the detrimental effects of anger. In other words, the Mikvah can help heal a person of their anger (*Sha'ar Ruach haKodesh*, Tikkun 15. *Kehilas Yaakov*, Ka'as. p. 755).

A *Gematria* / numerical equivalence is not mere coincidence, and the link between two equivalent concepts is often quite profound. Keep in mind that the numerical correlation is but an external indication of their inner relationship, not the source or the foundation of their relationship. A matching Gematria does not automatically suggest cosmological or theological equivalence, rather, it is an outward expression of a deeper cosmological truth that is already there (Ramban, *Sefer HaGeulah*, in the beginning. Rabbeinu Bachya, *Kad Kemach*, Tzitzis. *Shomer Emunim HaKadmon*, 1, 20-23). Sometimes, a numerical equivalency is the hidden key that unlocks and reveals the mystery.

To better understand the bond between Mikvah and dissolving anger, let us delve a bit deeper into the issue of anger, and observe why Mikvah is an appropriate *Tikkun* / means to extricate a person from the choke-hold of anger.

---

because most people who are angry use *words* to spew their anger (*Sha'ar haOsyos*, Kedushah, 12).

The 'Death' in Anger

Everyone recognizes the horrible and destructive nature of the *Midah* / trait of anger. One of the most often quoted teachings regarding anger is, "One who became angry is as if he served idols" (Rambam, *Hilchos De'os*, 2:3. *Teshuvas Harashbash*, Siman 370. *Zohar* 1, Berieshis, 2:16. See also *Shabbos*, 105b, where it states: "One who 'acts' upon their anger...," which is different than one who simply 'feels' anger, *Ma'haratz Chayos*, ad loc). And indeed, underlying every expression of anger is a hidden sense of heresy. In the act of becoming angry, we are ultimately saying that we reject the way the Creator's Light has become manifest. For instance, a person driving down the highway is cut off by another car. If the driver becomes angry, he is essentially enacting a kind of heresy, asserting that he rejects Hashem's plan and that he himself has a better idea of how things should happen.

This assertion exacerbates the sense of being 'cut off' from life and the Source of all life. Anger is in fact an *Aveirah* / transgression, literally a 'crossing over to the other side' of a divide that separates a person from the Creator. An Aveirah also divides you from your deeper self, and from Hashem's Creation as a whole.

Outwardly, acting out in anger may be most damaging to the recipient of the anger, but on a deeper level, anger harms the angry person as well. It ends up making a person do things, say things and certainly think things, that one would normally not do, say or think. "One who expresses anger is as if he lit the fires of *Gehenom* / hell" (*Tikkunei Zohar*, Tikkun 48. see *Nedarim*, 22a). All forms of torment, anguish and misery are opened up and ignited when a person feels and acts out of anger.

Anger robs a person of his true potential; he denies himself the ability to be the caring, loving person he can truly be. A person who is angry feels small, narrow, limited, constricted, small minded, and he projects this same image onto the people and the world around him. He begins to feel that the whole world is out to get him; that it is a bad, ugly, cruel world, and there is no room for hope, dreams or possibilities. In place of seeing the world with hope as the Creator does, "And Hashem saw that it was good," all one sees is negativity, strife and futility.

An angry person should not pray (*Eiruvin*, 65a. See Tosefos ad loc for the Biblical 'source'. *Tur*, Orach Chayim Siman 98. Today, however, he should nonetheless pray, *Shulchan Aruch*, Siman 98:2). Why? Because, on a deeper level, he literally 'cannot' pray while in a state of anger. He is not open to the condition of prayer; he has lost hope and therefore does not truly acknowledge the Infinite Presence of Hashem.

After many years of not seeing his beloved son Yoseph, and thinking he was not alive, Yaakov says, "I never *Philalti* that I would ever see your face again" (*Bereishis*, 48:11). What does *Philalti* mean? Rashi interprets Yaakov's statement to imply: 'I was so devastated by your absence that I never would have *filled my heart* to think the thought that I would ever see your face again.' The word *l'Hispalel*, which means to perform *Tefilah* / prayer, comes from the same root as does *Philalti*. Tefilah is thus to consciously fill our hearts and minds with hopes and dreams of what we truly desire to see — a world that is healed and perfected. To pray is to hope for a better and brighter reality, to imagine a sick person being healed, a broken hearted person feeling whole, and ultimately, to envision the entire world healing with the coming of Moshiach. For this reason, when a person is in a posture of anger, in which everything seems gloomy and morbid, with the inaccurate sense that there is no possibility of wellbeing or reconciliation in the future, they cannot pray. Without an accurate understanding of Hashem's world and its potential, we too cannot pray.

When we are angry, our entire perspective is blurred, and everything seems opaque and dark. As it says in Tehilim: "My eye is dimmed from anger" (*Tehilim*, 6:8. 31:10. *Iyov*, 17:7). Simply put, anger blinds a person, plaguing them with a total lack of clarity.

When a person cannot see, they cannot properly assess situations correctly. Sadly, in anger, one's reality is completely obscured. As a result, his actions are devastatingly reactionary. His vision narrows, his consciousness shrinks. A wise person forgets his wisdom in anger, and a prophet loses his Divine intuition (*Pesachim*, 66b). No matter who you are, whatever level of spirituality and consciousness you have achieved, you lose in anger. Everything essential to a person is lost in anger.

"An angry person", say our Sages, "is left with nothing other than his anger" (*Kidushin*, 41a). One's clarity of thought becomes clouded, and there is no wisdom. This loss of wisdom can even be understood on a physiological level. In anger, the body produces more adrenaline, temporarily giving the body a boost of strength and vitality to fight and protect itself, but, as a result, less blood flows to the brain. Since our brains get less oxygen, our thinking is less clear.

As a result, anger damages one's vision; it does not allow the person to see what is really going on right in front of him. When angry, you view the whole world through the lens of your anger; everything and everyone seems to be scheming to threaten your existence, your honor or your comfort.

Additionally, with anger comes a great deal of isolation; individual anger separates you from other individuals. Group anger separates that group from other groups. When a person feels angry 'because' a certain individual insulted him, his anger cuts him off from having open relationships with others, even those individuals he is most intimate with, such as his spouse, parents or children.

"There is no friendship or companionship in anger" says the wise 13th century sage, Rabbi Yedaya haPenini (*Mivchar haP-ninim*, 18:2). In anger, one feels isolated and lonely, and no one seems to be on his side. Such isolation, if not dealt with, can lead to deep mistrust and fear. Anger isolates a person even from himself: this is the most devastating effect.

Unchecked, unhealed anger metamorphs into a general state of lifelessness and depression. Depression can be understood as inwardly directed anger, or *anger without enthusiasm*. And once a person falls into this pit, it becomes difficult to lift them into any state of *Chayus* / connectivity, hope or freedom.

"An angry person, his life is not life" (*Pesachim*, 113b). The anger eventually leads to a type of inner 'death' and Tumah, severance from others, and from one's own self, leaving the person bereft of real vitality or appreciation of life.

Loss of Soul

As a result of anger, the *Chayus* / aliveness of a person leaves them, making them feel bitter and depleted. They are collapsed, not merely psychologically, but also spiritually. The holy Zohar tells us dramatically that a person who is angry 'loses his soul' (*Zohar* 2, p. 182b. *Sha'ar haGilgulim*, Hakdamah 5). Every other negative act or state affects a single area in the body. For instance, lying affects the mouth, and gazing at harmful imagery affects the eyes. However, anger affects the entire soul, which departs when a person is angry (*Sha'ar Ruach haKodesh*, p. 33).

When a person becomes angry their face turns red, and other colors as well, but most noticeably, after some time, it becomes pale and white. This change of skin tone is, from a metaphysical point of view, an external representation of an internal exhaustion and loss of Chayus, spirit and soul (*Maor vaShemesh*, Parshas Tazria). There is a tangible effect on the body when the soul, the inner life force of a person, is repelled by anger. What is needed in such a moment is a total purification, a radical enlivening of oneself, a complete expulsion of the Tumah and a powerful recovery of soul, of Teharah. This is the gift of the Mikvah.

Mikvah is spelled מקוה which can also be read as *Mi Kaveh* / *from* מקוה' / from hope. In the Torah, the word *Mikvah* is also used to mean 'hope'. In the book of Yirmiyahu (14:8) a verse says, מקוה ישראל מושיעו בעת צרה / "O **hope** of Israel, his Savior in a time of trouble." Mikvah is a place of *Tikvah* / hope. When we enter a Mikvah, it is an expression of hope in renewal and rebirth, as we are seeking to emerge again into a new form, filled with innocence, yearning, hope and dreams of a brighter future. By immersing in a Mikvah, we are reclaiming our Neshamah, our Infinity, which is linked forever with the power of the *Ohr Ein Sof* / Infinite Light of the Creator.

It is therefore within the cool, peaceful waters of the Mikvah that we regain our soul, which fled from the fires of our anger and the toxic smoke of our morbid depression. We need to return to a hopeful state of fluidity, movement and openness, in order to regain our lost soul (*Reishis Chochmah, Sha'ar haAhavah, 11*). After all, it was a rigid, stagnant, closed way of thinking and interacting with life which gave rise to our anger in the first place. As such, we need to treat the root cause, not just the symptom.

The Root of Anger

The root of all anger is the narrowness of ego, and its rigidity of thought and expectation. For the most part, anger arises from an arrogant belief that we know how life ought to look and how events should unfold.

Whenever we are stuck in an image of self, or fasten our imagination onto what we think is to be expected, we are sure to become angry. This is because life will never conform to our expectations, and our internal perception will invariably be disrupted. We construct mental images of who we are, how people should act toward us, and how events need to unfold. When the flow of life seems to veer from these constricted boundaries, we are jarred. 'How could this person say such a thing?' 'How could they do such a thing to me?' 'How can *this* happen to *me*?' All these are statements of an ego in distress over broken mental constructs and childish demands. Our fragile identity lives in perpetual fear of being interrupted. We become so reactive and sensitive that when someone 'tickles' us in the wrong way, we explode in anger.

When our ego dictates our perspective, we are constantly being hurt and are compelled to continually ask disingenuous questions, such as, 'Why is this happening to me?' And, 'Who do you think you are?' Since these are not actually questions but accusations, we can never receive a satisfying answer, and we become stuck in pointing our finger outwards at others and at the world. Really, the root and cause of our anger is not 'out there', it is 'in here', in our own stiffness, 'deadness' and Tumah.

A person who is morbidly stiff and unyielding needs to enter a Mikvah so that they can begin to operate in a paradigm of life, fluidity and flexibility.

A wealthy person "is one who has a bathroom next to his table" (*Shabbos*, 25b). Wealth is joy, as our Sages tell us: "Who is wealthy? The one who is joyous with what he has" (*Avos*, 4:1). In addition to the literal affluence and ease implied in having a restroom near your dining room, on a deeper level it means that a wealthy or joyous person is someone who is relaxed and trusting, open to receiving (table) and even immediately letting go (restroom). When we immerse ourselves in the Mikvah, we relax; we become so connected to the infinitely wealthy Source of Life, that we do not fear others taking our well-being away. If we notice any sensations of 'anger' arise, we immediately release them and return to the joyous feast of life.

Into the Ayin & the Name Ehe'yeh

Our ego is our *Ani* / small i, our rigid, reactive, stagnant self-identification as *Yesh* / some-thing-ness. To undo this Tumah-infused way of being and thinking, we need to enter the fluid, placid, undefined reality of the Mikvah waters. We need to enter Ayin / no-thing-ness and emptiness, so that we can emerge fresh and new into a fluid, non-reactive, healthy Ani. It is worth pointing out that Ani and Ayin are comprised of the same letters; they are in fact two halves of the same coin of consciousness.

In the process of trading in the false, small *i*, for the real *I*, the essence of who we really are, we first need to shed all self images; this is the state of Ayin. In order to reclaim and reconnect to our true identity, there is an intermediary transitional stage in which the false ego-image is no longer dominant, although we are not yet inhabiting the true, rectified image of our soul-potential. At this point, we are 'not-this' and 'not-that'; we are Ayin. Analogously, if you wish to make a table into a chair, you first need to deconstruct and disassemble the table and only then can you work on constructing the chair. For an object to change from what it is to what you desire it to become, there needs to be at least a moment when it ceases being what it was. We therefore need to first surrender and deconstruct the lower Ani image, allowing ourselves to become Ayin, and only then, from that place of imageless nothingness, can we begin to take on our new, true form of being. But first, we need to see through the emptiness of ego.

Once we are fully immersed in, and identify as, the Ayin of the Mikvah, we can begin to move from our utter image-less-ness towards our new, true self image. Therefore, at this point in the process, before emerging from the waters, we meditate on the Name *Ehe'yeh* / I will be. Before we break the surface and rise up from the water, we should try to visualize the letters of this sacred Name and meditate on what it means.

Mikvah, as mentioned, is 151 in numeric value. This is the same as the value of the filled Name Ehe'yeh (*Sha'ar haKavanos*, Erev Shabbos), meaning when each of the four letters in the Name *Ehe'yeh* (Aleph, Hei, Yud, Hei) are spelled out:
Aleph is spelled Aleph/1, Lamed/30, Pei/80 = 111
Hei is spelled Hei/5, Hei/5 = 10
Yud is spelled Yud/10, Vav/6. Dalet/4 = 20
Hei is spelled Hei/5, Hei/5 = 10
(111+10+20+10=151/*Mikvah*)*

---

* Another variation is to multiply the numbers: Aleph is 1, and 1x1=1. Hei

The Name *Ehe'yeh*, as explored previously, is related to the future, as in 'becoming'. *Ehe'yeh Asher Ehe'yeh* is often translated as, "I Am That I Am," but more accurately it means, "I will be what I will be." As Rashi comments on this name, Hashem is ultimately saying to Moshe: 'I will be with them (the Children of Israel) now, and I will be with them in their future, [however that may present itself]' (*Rashi*, Shemos, 3:14). With this name, Hashem is telling us: 'I am I, who can be (and deeply is) expressed in everything — in the present as 'Being' and in the future as 'Becoming''.

When we enter the fluid, transitional space of the holy Mikvah, we may focus on the Name Ehe'yeh. We thereby seek to connect through this name to the Divine *Koach* / power that engenders movement, transformation, and 'becoming' again the pure soul that we have lost. Through this name and the living waters of the Mikvah, we recover our Chayus by emptying ourselves of our anger and the false self-images that caused it, and then enclothing ourselves in freedom, positivity, generosity and joy.

Practically speaking, the next time you flare up in anger, whether at your parents, spouse, children, a co-worker, a stranger, or even against yourself or the world around you, go as soon as possible to a Mikvah.

---

is 5, and 5x5=25 [1+25=26]. Yud is 10, and 10x10=100 [1+25+100=126]. Hei is 5, and 5x5=25 [1+25+100+25=151] (*Sha'ar haPesukim*, Pinchas).

As you take off your garments, do so with presence and Kavanah. Remove each layer of Kelipah, of rigid assumption and expectation, feeling yourself getting progressively cooler, freer and lighter. Let your entire being be embraced in the peaceful, comforting waters of the Mikvah. Sense your self-image and narrative disappearing, as you are submerged in the world of Olam haBa, of radiant purity and new potential. Under the water, visualize the Name *Ehe'yeh* (א-ה-י-ה), and know that 'the One Who is Always Becoming' is giving you the Koach to become who you really are, and to engage in life in a wholesome, holy way.

CHAPTER 11

~~

How Many Immersions?

D UE TO THE NATURE OF SPIRITUAL METAMOR-
PHOSIS AVAILABLE THROUGH IMMERSING IN A
MIKVAH, WHICH IS MORE AKIN TO A QUANTUM
LEAP THAN A GRADUAL PROGRESSION, a single dip
contains all of the transformative power necessary to shift
one's state from Tamei to Tahor. However, in order to deep-
en one's Kavanah and experience of such a renewal, most
customs suggest a series of numerous, repetitive immersions, meaning to dunk a certain number of times before
exiting the Mikvah. For example, if you were to immerse
twice, you would use the first dunk to let go of whatever
you need to let go of — the hectic energy of the weekdays,
Tumah, or negative emotional states. Then, you would immerse a second time to assume your new state of Shabbos, purity or positivity. This pattern applies to any number
of immersions, and for all purposes. Yet, there is extensive
conversation among the *Poskim* / leading Halachic decid-
ers and *Mekubalim* / Kabbalists with regards to how many
immersions one performs on Erev Shabbos specifically. In
the following pages, we will explore the deeper meanings of
various numbers of Erev Shabbos Mikvah immersions. This
will equip the reader to make their own informed decisions
when immersing in a Mikvah before Shabbos.

Additionally, once we understand the intents and effects of
various numbers of Erev Shabbos immersions, we can then
draw parallels for Erev Yom Kippur immersions, as well as
all the other Mikvah practices explored in this book.

Number of Immersions on Erev Shabbos

There are various ways to contextualize and understand the practice of immersing in a Mikvah on Erev Shabbos in general, as well as the specific number of times one chooses to immerse. The different numbers of repetitions prescribed depend on the inner processes ascribed to such immersions, and what they represent, respectively. The prevalent customs range from one to ten immersions, although many sources suggest 13, 14, 39, 72, or even 310 immersions. What follows is a list of ten possible practices with their accompanying Kavanos. Keep in mind that these Kavanos should generally be meditated on when the body is completely submerged or 'covered' in the Mikvah.

One

It is most important to understand — a single immersion in the Mikvah fulfills the basic halachic requirements, and affords full transformative power. If you are immersing once on Erev Shabbos, as you are under the water, have the intention to release any trappings, bindings, residues or 'garments' from the work-week; let go of your mundane, utilitarian ways of thinking, speaking, acting and interfacing with the world around you. When Shabbos begins, these weekday garments will have been effectively removed and you will be ready to receive the *Kedushah* / transcendental holiness of Shabbos.

This single immersion practice is actually hinted at in the Zohar (2, 204a): "As Shabbos is approaching, the holy people need to clean themselves from the engagement with the work-week." Why? Because during the week, another form of spirit rests upon and hovers in this world, and when a human being wants to leave that spirit and elevate to a higher, holy spirit, they need to first clean themselves, so that the higher holy spirit can rest upon them (*Sidurei Shel Shabbos*, Shoresh Harishon).

Relatedly, the Baal Shem Tov once publicly guaranteed that if someone needed the Mikvah for any reason and was able to immerse only once, that one time would not harm them in any way. For example, if it were winter and one could only immerse in freezing water, or perhaps the water is not so hygienic or clean — then this single immersion would be covered by the 'insurance policy' of the Baal Shem Tov (*Baal Shem Tov, Torah*, Yisro, 15. The idea that a single immersion will not do any harm is also mentioned earlier by the *Reishis Chochmah*, Sha'ar haAhavah, 11). So confident in the spiritual powers of the Mikvah was the Baal Shem Tov, that he would encourage people to brave any and all elements and circumstances for even a single immersion.

Two

The Arizal speaks of immersing (at least) twice on Erev Shabbos: once to remove the spiritual garments of the weekday, and once to become 'dressed' within the holy garments of Shabbos (*Pri Eitz Chayim, Sha'ar haKavanos*).

On the first immersion, intend to remove and release your weekday focus and level of consciousness, and on the the second, intend to assume the consciousness and reality of the holy Shabbos. The Arizal also suggests that when you are under the water, 'bow' toward the west, and inwardly declare, 'I am immersing to rid myself of the garments of the weekday.' On the second submersion, bow and say, 'I am immersing to accept upon myself the holiness of Shabbos' (*Pri Eitz Chayim*, Sha'ar 18, Sha'ar haShabbos, 3. *Kanfei Yonah*, 3:45. *Siddur Shaloh*, Erev Shabbos, Tevilah. *Sha'ar haOsyos*, Kedushah, 9).

According to the Arizal, a Tzadik, or even a person who is temporarily in a higher state, may 'see' with his inner eye a type of vapor emanating from the tips of his fingernails and departing from his body during the first immersion. This subtle phenomenon is a reflection of the departing of the spirit of the weekday. As explored earlier, Kelipah is connected to the hands and collects itself, as it were, in the nails. This is one reason that we should trim our nails and wash our hands in hot water before Shabbos.

Three

The Ben Ish Chai (Rabbi Yosef Chaim of Baghdad, 1832-1909) specifies that we should immerse ourselves three times on Erev Shabbos. The first dunk is to cleanse our *Nefesh* / actions of the past work-week, the second to cleanse our *Ruach* / emotions and speech of the week, and the third to cleanse our *Neshamah* / intellect and thoughts of the week (*Ben Ish Chai*, Lech Lecha). At the same time that we are releasing those weekday energies, we should have the Kavanah that we are receiving the Nefesh, Ruach and Neshamah of Shabbos.

Another practice of three immersions: the first immersion is to remove the 'dirt' and the garments of the past week, and the two subsequent immersions correspond to *Na'aseh* / 'we will do what Hashem asks of us,' and *Nishmah* / 'we will listen and understand the Torah' (*Shaloh*, Meseches Shabbos, 88). These three immersions are also an appropriate practice for Teshuvah (*Shulchan Aruch haRav*, Orach Chayim. 606:11-12. See also *Kanfei Yonah*, 1:95. *Siddur Shaloh*, Erev Shabbos, Tevilah) on any day of the week, as we always need to release our negative actions, emotions, words and thoughts, and assume a posture of Na'aseh veNishmah.

Four

Shabbos is called *Yom laHashem* / a day to Hashem, or '... to the Name Yud-Hei-Vav-Hei'. As we are about to enter Hashem's world in a revealed and focused way on Shabbos, we immerse into the Mikvah four times, corresponding to the four letters of Hashem's Name. On the first immersion, contemplate the letter Yud, on the second, the letter Hei, on the third, the letter Vav, and on the fourth, the letter Hei. This was once a widespread practice (R. Alexander Ziskind, *Yesod Shoresh haAvodah*, Sha'ar 8:1).

The Divrei Chayim (Rabbi Chayim of Tzanz, 1793-1876) would immerse himself four times, corresponding to the four death penalties described in the Torah and revealed by our Sages. With each dunk he would imagine himself receiving one of the four forms of execution. This 'contemplative death practice' is similar to the practice suggested before one goes to sleep, in which one imagines that he has already passed on, having received all four forms of death penalty, thereby erasing all accumulated negativities and spiritual blemishes (*Yesod Shoresh haAvodah*, Derushei Kriyas Shema she'Al haMitah). Underwater, a person is in a state of *Ayin* / non-being, and experiences a death of sorts. The Divrei Chayim would harness this contemplative state to cleanse his soul and deeply experience a rebirth. Be assured that if you use this Kavanah vividly, you will rid yourself of all negative desires and pettiness, and emerge refreshed and renewed.

Five

We each possess five levels of soul. In addition to our *Nefesh* / vital animating energy, our *Ruach* / emotive consciousness, and our *Neshamah* / intellective faculties, we have two higher levels of soul, that are more transcendent: *Chayah* / life force or spiritual consciousness, and *Yechidah* / unity, or Divine consciousness. On the level of Yechidah, you are no longer separate from anything, and you are existentially submerged within the ultimate Unity of Hashem.

We find that the Cohen Gadol, the High Priest, immersed himself five times on Yom Kippur, as Yom Kippur is the *Achas baShanah* / oneness of time, and a day in which we connect with the oneness of consciousness, the level of Yechidah. (Indeed, every day, even a regular, pure Cohen would immerse five times before entering the Azarah, *Yumah*, 30a.)

Every Erev Shabbos is like a mini Erev Yom Kippur (*Beis Aaron*, Ki Tisa). Also, there are five levels of immersion in a Mikvah corresponding to five degrees of purity (*Chagigah*, 2:6). For these reasons, five is a good number of immersions on any occasion (the Rebbe, *Sha'arei Halacha uMinhag*).

When you immerse five times, have the intention that with each one you are garbing yourself with another dimension of soul and reaching a higher level of purity, first Nefesh, then Ruach, Neshamah, Chayah, and finally Yechidah, which is the everpresent stainless purity of your essence.

There are four sides or walls to the Mikvah, corresponding to the first four dimensions of the soul Nefesh, Ruach, Neshamah and Chayah. The midpoint of the Mikvah is that which unites all four dimensions, corresponding to the all-unifying 'dimension' of Yechidah.

There is a tradition of *Kavanos* / intentions for the daily Mikvah from the Baal Shem Tov, based on five Divine Names, which is recorded by his students and their students (*Pri haaretz*, Lech Lecha. *Chesed leAvraham.* p. 151. *Likutei Yekarim*, 27-28. See also *Siddur Im Dach,* Kavanas haMikvah). These Names, besides having metaphysical power to create unifications in the worlds above, also affect us and are related to us in a very real way.

-1-

With the first immersion, think about the Divine Name *Ehe'yeh.* The Name *Ehe'yeh* when filled, is numerically 151, equal to the value of the word *Mikvah.* As you are underwater, place your intention on the Name *Ehe-yeh*, representing the Divine potential of the future. Think about how nothing is etched in stone, and by connecting with the Source of All Life we can begin at any moment to create a more wholesome future. Notice in this moment underwater, how life is filled with infinite possibilities and processes of unfolding.

-2-

Before the second immersion, meditate on the Divine Name Ag'lah — a Name connected to *Gevurah* / restriction, power and might. This Name, Ag'lah, is found in the first letters of the words in the second blessing of the Amidah: *Ata Gibor Le'Olam Ado-noi* / "You are Mighty, (*Gibor* / Gevurah) forever Hashem." Now during the second immersion, have in mind that the Name *Ag'lah* (Aleph, Gimel, Lamed, Aleph) becomes the Name *Ei'led* (Aleph-Lamed-Dalet; the Aleph/1 and Gimel/3 from Ag'lah transform into the Dalet/4 of Ei'led). (Both these Names have the same numeric value of 35, and are thus interconnected. Siddur *Sha'ar haShamayim*, "Ata Gibor".) The Divine Name Ei'led is the tenth of the 72 Names of Hashem* and it is associated with the quality of *Chesed* / Loving-kindness. Literally, the word *Ei'led* means 'I will be born'. By meditating on this process from Gevurah to Chesed, one acknowledges that by immersing in the Mikvah — 'I am being recreated'. The name Ei'led breaks through and sweetens all the Gevurah and limitations in your life, thereby opening up the possibility to give birth to new vistas of possibility. All this and more is able to be achieved through focused awareness, higher understanding

---

* In the book of Shemos (14:19-21) there are three consecutive verses, which each contain 72 letters. The letters of these three verses can be arranged as 72 triplets of letters. The first verse is written out in sequence, each letter separate from the next. The second verse is to be written in reverse order, from the last letter to the first. Each letter of the second verse is then paired with a corresponding letter from the first verse. For example, Vav is the first letter of the first verse, and Hei is the last letter of the second verse, so the Hei is paired with the Vav. Next, the third verse is written out in sequence, and these letters are now paired with the two previous letters. So, the third verse begins with a Vav thus the first name of the 72 Names is Vav-Hei-Vav.

and the living waters of the Mikvah; essentially, everything can be transformed in higher understanding.

-3-

During the third immersion meditate only on the Name Ei'led; consider how the act of connecting with this Name connects us with the Source of All Life, thereby giving us the power to birth and be birthed into a new reality. Not only is there 'potential' in this name, as the Name Ehe'yeh represents; the Name Ei'led has the added ability to 'actualize', to manifest the potential. If Eh'yeh is the power to become pregnant with infinite possibility, Ei'led is the power of birth itself.

Because of this very power to transform constriction into expansion, the students of the Baal Shem Tov teach (*Degel Machanei Ephrayim*, Vayera) that a woman in labor, or who wants to begin labor, should meditate on the Name Ei'led. As explained, this is the Divine name connected with actually giving birth.

As mentioned above, *Ei'led* is spelled Aleph, Lamed, Dalet. These three letters embody the entire structure of the Ten Sefiros,* the Divine flow from *Keser* / 'crown' all the way

---

* There are Ten *Sefiros* / basic Divine Attributes. These are like ten screens through which the Infinite Light of Hashem creates, penetrates and reveals itself within finite reality. The word *Sefirah* (plural, *Sefiros*) comes from the word *Lispor* / 'to count'; as in, a numeration, a finite numbering (*Pardes Rimonim*, Sha'ar 1:1. *Yahel Ohr*, 6d). It is also related to the word *S'far* / 'edge', as in the edge of a city. Each Sefirah is

until *Malchus* / majesty, the receiver. Here is the process: Aleph, 'the One', represents Keser, the highest level of Divine manifestation. In the Name Ei'led the Aleph moves into the Lamed. The shape of the Lamed contains three lines, reflecting the three columns of Sefiros, right, left and middle. The right column is comprised of *Chochmah* / wisdom, *Chesed* / kindness, and *Netzach* / victory. The left column is *Binah* / understanding, *Gevurah* / strength, and *Hod* / humility. The middle column is *Da'as* / awareness, *Tiferes* / compassion, and *Yesod* / connection. The light of the Aleph of *Keser* thus moves down through the Lamed, representing the nine Sefiros, and from there into the letter Dalet, which represents the four dimensions or directions of the World of Malchus.

Rabbi Moshe Dovid Valli writes (*Sefer haLikutim* 2, p. 635), that the Divine Name Ei'led is what gives Malchus the power to reveal and distribute her flow to the lower realms. *Ei'led* draws down from the 'place' of Keser (which is connected to the Name *Ehe'yeh*), the place of pure potential, into the Ten Sefiros, where the potential begins to actualize, until the *Shefa* / flow enters the womb, the receiver of Malchus. Then Malchus gives birth.

---

a measurable 'edge' of the One Light; they thus allow the Infinite Light to appear 'measured' and bordered. The word *Sefirah* is also related to the word *Sipur* / 'story' (*Sefer Yetzirah*). The Sefiros are like a linear story about the Infinite Light. Finally, the Sefiros are *Sappir* / 'illuminations', like glowing sapphires (*Zohar Chadash*, Yisro, 41b. see Rebbe Rashab, *Hemshech Ayin Beis* 1, p. 159).

-4-

During the fourth immersion, one creates a union of Ehe'yeh and Ei'led. When your head is underwater, create a *Shiluv* / a mental-visual unity between these two Divine Names. To do this, in your mind's eye, spell the Name *Ehe'yeh* in its full *Milu'im* / expanded form — spelling the letters themselves: Aleph-Lamed-Pei, Hei-Hei, Yud-Vav-Daled, Hei-Hei. Now, intersperse the three letters of the Name *Ei'led*, Aleph, Lamed and Dalet, within the expanded spelling of Ehe'yeh, as follows: Aleph-Lamed-Pei-**Aleph** — Hei-Hei-**Lamed** — Yud-Vav-Dalet-**Dalet** — Hei-Hei. If you can, gaze at this image of the unity of these two Names, written out in your mind's eye as one long Name. As explained, *Ehe'yeh* / 'I will be' is the potential of birth, and *Ei'led* is the actual ability to give birth. Therefore the *Shiluv* of these two names is 'the possibility and actual ability to conceive and give birth to a new reality'.

During this fourth immersion, you should pray for what you truly desire, what you want to 'give birth' to. Know that the 'possibility' is there, and you can, by connecting to the Source of All Life, receive the 'ability' to give birth to and actualize a new reality.

-5-

On the fifth immersion, create a simpler Shiluv between the Name Ehe'yeh and the Name Ei'led. Take the letters of *Ehe'yeh* (not written out in full, just the four basic letters

Aleph-Hei-Yud-Hei) and intersperse them with the three letters of *Ei'led*: Aleph-**Aleph**-Hei-**Lamed**-Yud-**Dalet**-Hei.

Keep in mind that all these Kavanos should be contemplated while the entire body is covered by the waters of the Mikvah (*Kaf haChayim*, Orach Chayim, 75:28).

The above five Kavanos, based on the teachings of the Baal Shem Tov, are quite lofty and complex. Let's look at it in a simpler, more 'psychological' way of activating this process:

-1-

First immersion: meditate on the Divine Potentiality (Ehe'yeh) that allows you to 'become', to change, to conceive.

-2-

Second immersion: meditate on the constrictions in your life, such as any frustrations or blockages in your financial life, your family life or other relationships, your physical health, or your spiritual life. Then, recognize that creating anything in your life is similar to birthing a child, in that it requires constriction and contractions. Consider that the difficulties you may be having are growing pains, and indications that you are about to give birth to something much greater. "According to the pain is the reward (the pleasure)" (*Avos*, 5:23). Pray and connect with Hashem, the All-Generous Source of Life, to move beyond these necessary constrictions and contractions in a fruitful and positive way.

-3-

Third immersion: bring to mind the Name Ei'led. Visualize the new reality that you want to birth and bring into being. While connecting to the power of the Name Ei'led, imagine what is already about to be birthed in actuality. (Don't be afraid: This Name is also a protection against negative influences, such as the *Ayin Harah* / evil eye. So be bold in your visualizations and prayers at this potent moment.)

-4-

Fourth immersion: think about the unity of the Name Ehe'yeh, 'I will become', and the Name Ei'led, 'I will birth'. The Infinite possibility can and will become an actual reality.

-5-

Fifth immersion: again, meditate on these two Names, but this time sense that the new reality that you prayed for is being born at this very moment, even as you are in the Mikvah.

This five-immersion practice is the most elaborate and detailed Kavanah that we will discuss.

Six

On Shabbos, we receive an extra measure of Nefesh, Ruach and Neshamah. If we immerse six times in the Mikvah, the first immersion is to cleanse our *Nefesh* / actions of the past mundane week, to remove the garments of the Nefesh. The second immersion is to cleanse our *Ruach* / emotions and speech of the past week, to remove the negative garments from our Ruach. The third is to cleanse our *Neshamah* / intellect, and thoughts of the past week, and negative garments from our Neshamah. The fourth is to accept upon ourselves and be enveloped in the new Shabbos Nefesh, a higher way of being and acting. With the fifth immersion, we accept upon ourselves and are enveloped in the Ruach of Shabbos, with a higher or deeper way of feeling and a more refined manner of speaking. And with the sixth immersion, we accept upon ourselves and are enveloped in the Neshamah of Shabbos, a deeper way of thinking and using our minds.

In this way, with each subsequent immersion, we can have the intention of first removing the garments of the mundane week and then enveloping ourselves in the new Nefesh-Ruach-Neshamah of Shabbos.

Seven

As Shabbos is the seventh day, many immerse seven times: six times to remove the garments of each of the six past weekdays, and the seventh to receive the new garments, and second, higher soul of Shabbos. Before your first immersion, think about your past Sunday and all that happened on it — your experiences, your impressions, your thoughts, feelings, frustrations, anxieties and interactions. As you descend below the surface of the water, let go of all the hardship and baggage, the 'garments', that might still be weighing you down from that day.

After going through all six days of the week in this way, pausing before each immersion to remember the events of the corresponding day, you have now arrived at the threshold of Shabbos. Contemplate the wonderful light of Shabbos that is about to suffuse your world, and as you submerge for the seventh time, become enveloped with the *Kedushah* / holiness of Shabbos (Note: *Kaf haChayim*, 260:4-6. *Ben Ish Chai,* Lech Lecha, 16). Totally let go of all your worries from the past week, let them dissolve in the Mikvah, and assume an inner posture of Shabbos, in which *Kol Melachtecha Asuya /* "All your work is done" (*Tur*, Orach Chayim from *Mechilta d'Rebbe Yishmael*, Yisro, 7. *Rashi*, Shemos, 20:9). Realize: 'Not only is all my work of the past week done, and there is nothing else for me to do or think about right now, but there is in fact no future work to be done at all. Shabbos is about to arrive and I am already aware that everything is eternally perfect and complete!'

Eight

On Shabbos, we celebrate the present moment of being alive. We also commemorate and experience the 'past': the primordial events of Creation, the liberation and going out of Egypt, and the revelation and receiving of Torah. But we also celebrate the future, a time when every day will be like Shabbos; in fact, Shabbos is a manifestation of *Olam haBa* / the World to Come within *Olam haZeh* / this world right here, right now (*Berachos*, 57b. *Mechilta*, Shemos, 31:13). Eight is the number associated with the World to Come. Seven represents the natural cycle of time and creation, such as the seven days of the week. Eight, which is one (or infinitely) beyond seven, represents a reality 'above' the cycle of time, this is the transcendent world of unity and freedom. Immersing eight times before Shabbos thus suggests enveloping oneself with the reality of the World to Come.

To perform this Kavanah, begin with the seven immersion practice above. With the first six immersions, shed the garments of the week that has passed, and with the seventh immersion, become enveloped within the holiness and wholeness of Shabbos. On the eighth immersion, prepare yourself to be garbed in the transcendent freedom and Kedushah of the World to Come.

Nine

The word *Shabbos* (Shin-Beis-Tav) in *Mispar Katan* / small numeric value is 9 (Shin/3 + Beis/2 + Tav/4 = 9). Nine is the number of *Emes* / truth (Aleph/1 + Mem/4 + Tav/4 = 9). As an illustration of this truthfulness, nine is always consistent and true to itself. This is expressed mathematically in the fact that nine multiplied by any number always yields a number whose digits add up to 9. For example, 9x2=18 (1+8=9); 9x3=27 (2+7=9); 9x4=36 (3+6=9). Shabbos is a time of truth, and even someone who is not normally trusted to speak truthfully is trusted on Shabbos. Even a simple or coarse person will not lie on Shabbos (*Yerushalmi,* Demai, 4:1). As we immerse ourselves in the Mikvah nine times, we can have the Kavanah to remove all the garments of *Sheker / falsehood* and garb ourselves within the Emes and holiness of Shabbos. As we emerge from the water, we assume the spiritual garments of deepest authenticity.

לב טהור ברא לי אלקים ורוח נכון חדש בקרבי / "Create in me a pure heart, O G-d, and renew within me an upright spirit" (*Tehilim,* 51:12). This nine-word verse is intricately connected with Mikvah and purity. In fact, the first letter of the first three words — Lamed (for *Lev*), Tes (for *Tahor*), and Beis (for *Bara*) — spell the word *Tovel* / immerse. The final letters, Beis, Reish, Aleph, spell the word *Bara* / created (Arizal, *Sha'ar haLikutim,* ibid. Shaloh, *Sha'ar haOsyos,* Teharah, 11). When we Tovel in the waters of the Mikvah we become a new, pure-hearted creation.

As there are nine words in this verse, a Kavanah for immersing nine times is to have in mind the corresponding word of the verse for each immersion. With the first immersion focus on the word *Lev* / heart, the second *Tahor* / pure, third *Bara* / create, etc.

Ten

The Chasam Sofer (Rabbi Moshe Schreiber/Sofer, 1762-1839) would immerse ten times in a Mikvah on Erev Shabbos. The Chidah (Rabbi Chayim Yoseph David Azulai, 1724-1806) also records the practice of immersing ten times on Erev Shabbos, with specific intentions (*Avodas ha-Kodesh*, Moreh beEtzbah, 1:10). Here are those intentions:

The first immersion is to remove the negativity of the week in general, and specifically any spiritual impurities that are attached to a male body due to wasteful emission of seed.

The second, third, fourth and fifth immersions correspond to the four death penalties mentioned in the Torah (See the practice of the Divrei Chayim, in "Four", above). These, in turn, correspond to the four letters in the Name of Hashem that manifest in our life. These four letters/dimensions may have been damaged by our actions during the week. With every dip, when we cease breathing, we are experiencing a minor form of death to atone for the damage we have caused on each of those four letters/levels of Divinity, in creation, and within our own soul. This Kavanah breaks down the walls of the ego, which creates the opportunity for a holy rebuilding of the self and the healing of the four letters.

The sixth immersion is intended to create a union within the four letters/levels of the Name of Hashem.

The seventh immersion is meant to annul all the negativity and spiritual damage that may have been created specifically through anger.

The eighth immersion is to remove any residue of our thoughts, words and actions from the week that may still subtly hold us down.

The ninth and tenth immersions are for the purpose of becoming completely enveloped within the infinite light, healing and holiness of Shabbos.

These are the most basic opinions regarding how many times a person should immerse in the Mikvah on Erev Shabbos.

Each person can choose what practice works best for them, and that itself can fluctuate and change from week to week depending on the situation and the state of consciousness one is in. For example, one week a person may feel that he was too exposed to, or marred by, the falsehood of the world and be drawn to immersing nine times in order to counteract the Sheker of the past week. On another week, he may desire the comprehensive soul-renewal of the five-immersion practice of the Baal Shem Tov. Our intention is not to prescribe any one of these practices in particular, but merely to inform the reader so that they have Torah-based options and authentic opinions to deepen their Mikvah experience.

One to Ten Immersions for Mikvah on Any Day

Many of the above Erev Shabbos practices can apply to any day of the week, or in fact to any other reason for immersion; and again, your choice of practice and approach can fluctuate or even change from day to day. Below are examples of one to ten immersion practices adjusted for days other than Erev Shabbos.

A single immersion practice for any given day would again be with the Kavanah of letting go and emptying yourself of all that is holding you down, all the Tumah or stagnation in your life and your egoic identity. Whether you are entering the Mikvah upon awakening in the morning, or after a flare-up of anger, or for any other reason, the objective of the single immersion is to totally let go and simply be free. A two-immersion practice would again be intended to first let go of, and remove, all residual negativity or impurity that one has accumulated, and then with the second immersion, to accept upon oneself the new spiritual energies and garments of purity and holiness. Essentially, every Mikvah practice has these two elements — the negation of the Tumah, and the activation of Teharah as you return to the world (*Tzafnas Paneach*, Hilchos Matnas Aniyim). Immersing twice allows you to engage these two elements individually, and thus more consciously and deliberately.

Three immersions are intended to first cleanse your *Nefesh* / vital energies and actions, then to cleanse your *Ruach* / emotions and speech, and finally to cleanse your *Neshamah* / intellect and thoughts. Desire and pray that Hashem will transform your ways of being, doing, feeling, speaking and thinking; that your actions should be more just, your emotions more rectified, and your thoughts more clarified. This three-part renewal will empower you to be and do your best in your quest to elevate and refine the fallen, hidden sparks in the world, and in coming ever closer to your loved ones and to Hashem.

It is brought down in the name of Rabbi Yehudah haChassid (1150-1217) that we should immerse three times in the Mikvah on Erev Yom Kippur, corresponding to the three descriptions that the Torah employs for 'transgression': *Cheit* / unintentional misdeeds, *Avon* / intentional transgressions, and *Pesha* / negative actions done in spite.*

---

* Corresponding to the three times the word *Teharah* / purity appears in the Torah portion that describes the Yom Kippur service. (*Vayikra*,

Yet, on any given day, we can also contemplate these three basic categories, and with each immersion we can have the intention to untangle ourselves from, and throw off one of these forms of negativity. Rabbi Yehudah haChassid also brings down (*Sefer Chassidim*, 394) that the common custom among women, after completing a Nidah period, is to immerse three times.

With four immersions you may intend to repair and become enveloped within each of the letters of the Four Letter Name of Hashem, perhaps imagining one of the letters in your mind's eye with each immersion (*Menoras HaZahav*, Metzorah. *Regel Yishara* [Dinov], Ma'areches Mem, Mikvah). Doing so will help you to get in touch with the injunction of *Shivisi Hashem leNegdi Tamid* / "I place 'the Name' before me at all times." This means simply to sense that your entire life, including all its ups and downs, is *Nochach Pnei Hashem* / in the immediate presence of Hashem.

Five immersions in the Mikvah correspond to the five levels of soul. With the first immersion in the Mikvah, open yourself to receive a cleansed and purified Nefesh, so your

---

16:19-30. *Sefer Chassidim*, 394. *Reishis Chochmah*, Sha'ar haAhavah, 11). Additionally, the word Mikvah appears in the Torah exactly three times: Bereishis 1:10, Shemos 7:10, and Vayikra 11:36. Many sources speak about these three immersions on Erev Yom Kippur (*Sefer Rokeach*, Yom Kippur, 214. Shulchan Aruch, Orach Chayim, *Magen Avraham*, 606:8. *Shulchan Aruch haRav*, 606:12. *Aruch haShulchan*. ibid. *Mishna Berurah*, ibid).

actions in this world will be holy and noble. With the second immersion, receive a cleansed and refined Ruach, so your emotions will be balanced and healthy. With the third immersion, receive a cleansed and transparent Neshamah, so that your thoughts and inner dialogue will be clear, focused and accurate. With the fourth immersion, open up to your Chayah, your spiritual self, so that you will be attuned to the will and desire of the Creator. With the fifth immersion, allow your Yechidah to be revealed, so that you will live with deep authenticity, fearlessly and faithfully being who you are meant to be in this life, and fulfilling your *Tikkun* / your soul's purpose in this world.

Six immersions are intended to refresh and reanimate your three personal soul levels, Nefesh, Ruach and Neshamah; the first set of three immersions is meant to release whatever obstructs or obscures your fullness on each of these three levels, and the second set of three immersions is an opportunity for you to accept upon yourself the commitment to act, speak and think in ways that are elevating and liberating for yourself and others.

Seven immersions correspond to the seven basic *Midos* / emotional attributes of the macrocosmic and microcosmic human being: *Chesed* / kindness and giving, *Gevurah* / strength and restriction, *Tiferes* / beauty and compassion, *Netzach* / victory and perseverance, *Hod* / thankfulness and humility, *Yesod* / foundation and connection, and *Malchus* /

majesty and receptivity. With each immersion we can rectify one of these traits/Sefiros. For example, nullify the lust and self-centered attachments of distorted Chesed, and allow rectified Chesed, which expresses healthy forms of sharing and love that consider the needs of others, to manifest actively in your life.

Eight is transcendence. You can therefore add an eighth immersion to the seven above in order to acknowledge the fact that what you are in essence transcends both distortion and rectification. Accept the fact that you are always already infinite and whole — both beyond and including all dualities and dichotomies.

Nine, as we have explored, is the symbol of *Emes* / truth. Every day of our lives, it is important that we expunge from our system the falsehood of this world, the influence of the *Alma d'Shikra* / the world of lies, and position ourselves to live with deep honesty.

The Lubavitcher Rebbe privately suggested to a certain person that he immerse nine times, in three sets of three. Physically, each set of three immersions begins and ends with a regular dip, bending and lowering the body vertically into the water; but the middle immersion should be in the position of a 'fish', meaning that the body assumes a horizontal posture with hands and feet spread out (*Otzar haChassidim*, b'Rachvei Tevel, p. 99). As mentioned, a fish is 'one with the water' — and everything that the water embodies and symbolizes — dynamic fluidity, primordial unity, and rejuvenative vitality.

Ten: In addition to the seven basic Midos, there are also three primary forms of higher intelligence, *Chochmah* / wisdom and intuition, *Binah* / reason and cognition, and *Da'as* / practical knowledge and awareness. Together, the seven and three form the Ten Sefiros / Divine Attributes, as reflected in the *Tzurah* / form of the human being, the archetypal microcosmic persona, the inner structure of the body and soul of creation. When we immerse ten times in the Mikvah, we can have the intention of cleansing our entire being and going through a total reset and renewal of body, self and soul.

In addition to these ten possibilities for a general Mikvah practice, there are also customs of immersing 13, 14, or more times. Using such variations might depend on the specific time or need of the moment. For example, on a fast day, or a day of special prayers, some people immerse thirteen times, corresponding to the 13 Attributes of Mercy (*Ateres Tiferes, Keser Malchus* (Ben Ish Chai), Siman 198). Immersing 14 times corresponds to the 14 (of the 28) *Itim* / 'times' of life (*Maavar Yabok*, Sefas Emes, 13), which the book of Koheles mentions. There are 14 positive 'times' of life and 14 negative times, such as, "a time to laugh and a time to cry...." For the purpose of Teshuvah, the custom is to immerse 14 times to rid oneself of the 14 negative Itim, and return back to the 14 positive Itim (Shaloh, *Sha'ar haOsyos*, Kedushah, 11).

Some have a custom to immerse 39 times, 72 times, and others even 310 times. The number 39 alludes to the 39 *Malkus* / lashes of the Torah. The number 72 refers to the 72-letter name of G-d, as well as to the Divine quality of Chesed, which numerically equals 72; Chesed, as we have learned, is intimately related to the life-giving nature of water. In Hebrew, the number 310 is represented by the letters Shin (300) and Yud (10), which are the letters that comprise the word *Yesh* / egoic existence, self or something-ness. 310 is also the numeric value of the word *Keri* / wasteful emission of seed, one of the original halachic reasons to immerse. The custom to immerse 310 times is thus intended to very vividly fulfil the basic Kavanah of Mikvah: to create a *Bitul haYesh* / a nullification or transparency of one's ego or fixed sense of self (*Malchei b'Kodesh* [Zlotshov], p. 173).

No matter how many immersions you perform, the main thing is to ensure that you are not still holding onto your Tumah, your smallness, your anger, your negative actions, narratives or images. You need to let go of these mentally to the best of your current ability in order to let go of them physically and spiritually. If you do not, in the language of our Sages, you are "immersing with a *Sheretz* / pest in your hand". Teharah and transformation do not occur if you immerse while willfully grasping onto the very item that made you impure.

We therefore have to enter the Mikvah with a posture of Teshuvah (*Reishis Chochmah*, Sha'ar haAhavah, 11); we need to viscerally feel a strong desire to change, to grow, to live higher and pray deeper, to let go of and move beyond all that is holding us back. For this process to work, we must be willing to cease from all our previous negative patterns of consciousness and behavior. And ultimately, to really be open to the transformational power of the Mikvah, we need to believe with a perfect Emunah / faith that all of this is truly possible, and that we deserve to be happy, healthy, truly holy and free to be who we are meant to be.

~~~

CHAPTER 12

~~~

Specific Kavanos

For Women; Post-Nidah and To Conceive

For Conversion

Before Yom Kippur

Every Day

Erev Shabbos

F YOU HAVE READ THIS FAR, YOU SHOULD HAVE A GOOD WORKING UNDERSTANDING OF THE DEPTHS of this most wonderful, transcendent, yet practical Mitzvah. You can, we hope, at the very least appreciate the nature and power of water to revitalize and rejuvenate, to shed the old and be birthed into the new. What follows is a collection of more condensed Kavanos, presented plainly, without all the 'theory', for some of the main functions of the Mikvah.

To fully understand and embody the inner meanings of each of these Kanavos, it will help to read and re-read, learn and re-learn, all that was explored in the previous chapters. Here, we will provide just the most basic descriptions of these practices, certainly not exhaustive overviews. Nor are these the 'only' Kavanah available for these kinds of immersions. But these suggestions, along with the previous chapters, should give the attentive reader more than enough to put into practice and deepen their Mikvah experience.

Each of the following practices shares a common 'foundation' and has three 'stages'. That foundation is the essential fact that Mikvah is a Mitzvah, and specifically one that that is a *Chok* / suprarational Mitzvah, which is transcendent of the world of rationality, and linked directly to the Source of All Life. Thus, when we enter a Mikvah, we are revealing and forging a meaningful link between ourselves and the Creator of All Life, even if it doesn't seem to make rational sense. This is the fundamental foundation of all Mitzvos,

and it is the basic Kavanah required in performing them.*
We need to keep this basic Kavanah in mind when we immerse in a Mikvah.

These are the three 'stages' of each Mikvah practice described below: 1) standing on the floor of the Mikvah, 2) immersing completely, 3) emerging from the water. It is also important to note that even before step 1, every Mikvah practice actually begins with removing one's physical garments, which inwardly corresponds to ridding oneself of mental and emotional heaviness, so that one's Kavanah in the Mikvah can be clear. Still, these 3 steps as outlined above are the primary points in the process to be aware of.

In step one, when you are standing on the floor of the Mikvah, there is an opportunity to meditate on where you are in your life in this moment. Ask yourself: what is your *Tzurah* / form, and what do you need to release? In step two, when you are submerged underwater, there is a release and loss of that defined Tzurah, and you become nullified in the world of pure potential. In step three, as you are emerging from the Mikvah, you are Tahor and empowered to live your <u>highest truth </u>and take on a new Tzurah.

---

* In fact, there are five grades of immersion, and for the higher grade, Kavanah is essential (Mishnah *Chagigah*, 2:6). *M'deRabanan* / from the perspective of our Sages, one who immerses to eat Terumah, Kodesh or Chatas, must have Kavanah. Although, according to Din Torah even without Kavanah the immersions are sufficient (Rambam, *Hilchos Avos haTumos*, 13:2; this seems to be derived from the Gemara, *Kesef Mishnah*, ad loc).

Women: Post Nidah

Nidah is both a time of 'mourning', of being more or less alone, and also a time of awakening deeper longing and desire for new life. It creates a temporary physical separation between spouses, allowing both partners to have their individual space within the marriage, while simultaneously it is a time in which desire for closeness is aroused.

Contemplate this wonderful Mitzvah and opportunity to reconnect, consciously and beyond rationality, with the Source of all Life and Giving. Focus on spiritually, mentally and emotionally preparing to be at one with your spouse, in purity and sanctity, and to reveal true *Shalom Bayis* / harmony and peace in the home.

Step One: think about where you are presently in your life, within yourself, within your marriage, as mother or daughter, and as a *Sh'luchah* / representative of Hashem.

Have the intention to rid yourself of all Tumah, along with any negative baggage you may be carrying, especially having to do with your marriage or family. Maybe there is a little lack of *Shalom Bayis* / peace in your home, or maybe there is a 'deadness' or distance between you and your spouse, think about how you want to let go of any grudges, hurt, judgments or limitations on your ability to connect.

Step Two: Immerse fully in the unifying holy waters of the Mikvah. When you are submerged, feel one with the water, let go of and become nothing so that you can receive everything. Sense the infinite waters surrounding and supporting you to achieve your full potential of aliveness, sensitivity, presence and intimacy.

Step Three: As you are rising through the surface of the water in your final immersion, have Kavanah to reconnect to your life with 'purity', to reconnect with your spouse, to reconnect with your deepest self, to your Divine mission in the world, and to the woman you want to become and know you can be.

~~~

Women: To Conceive

Often, the post-Nidah Mikvah immersion is also a moment right before conception, G-d willing. Thus, it is a time to consciously connect to the Source of All Life and open up to creating new life, drawing down wonderful souls into soon-to-be-conceived children. Here is a short Kavanah for opening to conception with *Kedushah* / holiness and *Teharah* / purity.

Step One: As you are standing in the Mikvah, establish a Kavanah and pray that Hashem should remove all Tumah and any physical, mental or spiritual blockages that may be holding you and your spouse back from conceiving.

If there are any blockages in you, resolve to let go of them. Commit to being more present, focused, open and truly intimate with your beloved.

Step Two: As you are submerging into the living waters, let go of any negative doubts, anxious thoughts, or stifling beliefs that conception is not possible. Completely let go of all your woes and worries. *Daven* / pray that the *Koach* / power of the *Ein Sof* / Infinite One that is present within these waters should empower you to draw a pure soul down into a new, healthy body, to be a finite vessel for the infinite creativity of the Creator of Life.

When you are in a fluid state, at one with the energy of water, you can flexibly and faithfully make space within yourself to receive, hold, carry, grow and birth a new creation.

Feel the Mikvah embracing you, unify with the primordial waters of Creation, tap into and resonate with the deep desire of the Creator to create life; feel the compassionate waters preparing and carrying you, giving you strength to conceive and nurture a child.

Step Three: As you are emerging from the Mikvah, know deeply that 'on a spiritual plane' you are already a mother. Stay focused as you get dressed and make your way home. As best as you can, hold onto this energy, fill your mind and heart with pure positivity and love, indulge only pure, holy images and narratives, at least until after you are together with your spouse.

Although both of the above Kavanos are intended for women, and the Torah's Mitzvah to immerse post-Nidah before intimacy is exclusively for women, there are many men who have a custom to also immerse in a Mikvah before intimacy. The above Kavanos can be easily modified for a man, should he choose to take on such a meritorious practice.

For Conversion

A true convert is a person born with a soul that is already connected on a concealed level to the Jewish people, who at some point 'rediscovers' and 'returns' to life as an open Jew. Thus, a convert is called a "convert who converts", they already had a soul-connection to Torah and Mitzvos even before conversion, since they, too, stood at Sinai (Chida, *Midbar Kadmos,* Gimel); this soul-connection just needed to go through a process of self-revelation, physical embodiment and halachic/communal recognition. However, in addition to this transformation into living according to *Halacha /* Jewish law, the 'new' convert is, in fact, gifted with a higher level of soul, one which is directly linked to the Tree of Life. This gift is received at the time of immersing in the Mikvah of conversion. Here is a 3-part Kavanah for conversion immersion.

Step One: Standing in the waters of the Mikvah, think about where you are presently in your life. Think about how you lived your life previously, until you found the ways of Torah and Mitzvos. Consider how you perhaps felt out of place or that something was missing in your life, and perhaps how you had a peculiar affinity to Jewish life and Jewish People. As you stand in the Mikvah about to immerse, gather together all of your life up until this point. Resolve to completely let go of your old way of life, and to open yourself to become a part of Klal Yisrael, with all the responsibilities and challenges that this might entail.

Step Two: Immerse fully in the re-birthing waters of the Mikvah. When you are utterly submerged, sense all the Tumah of your past completely relaxing, releasing, relinquishing and dissolving. You are now attached to *Elokim Chayim* / the Living G-d of Israel, the Torah of Life and the Eternal People.

Step Three: As your head is moving up out of the water in the final immersion have the Kavanah that you are like "a child that is just born" (*Yevamos*, 97b), a new Neshamah with a new beginning. Feel invigorated, empowered and prepared to live as a Torah-committed Jew, with excitement, love and awe.

~~~~~

Before Yom Kippur

Yom Kippur is our collective day of *Teshuvah* / return and transformation. It is the day of *Emes* / truth*, a day that we need to enter with utmost authenticity and presence. The process of Teshuvah on Yom Kippur allows for the deepest truth of who we are, and who we can become, to be revealed.

As we are about to enter this awesome and holy day, we should prepare by immersing in the Mikvah in a heightened mood of Teshuvah.

Step One: Standing in the waters of the Mikvah, think about where you are in life this very moment. Practice *Hachna'ah* / submission; accept and acknowledge the patterns and products of your thoughts, words and actions. Honestly answer the question, 'Am I living authentically?' Take a personal accounting and assume full responsibility for your current state of being.

Think through the past year, and focus on your failings and mistakes, your negative actions, words or ways of thinking, whether intentional or unintentional. Resolve to truly let go of all these negative tendencies, to let go of your inauthentic patterns of behavior.

---

* Rosh Hashanah is a time of *Din* / judgment, Yom Kippur is a time of *Emes* / truth, and Sukkos is "the third pillar upon which the world stands": *Shalom* / peace.

Commit to rectifying them and to returning to wholesomeness and holiness as many times as necessary during the coming year, until you are fully living as the person you want to become.

Step Two: Immerse yourself fully in the transformative waters of the Mikvah. While you are under the water, completely let go of all your accumulated negativity. As you are floating and merging within the fluidity of the water, sense all of that Tumah simply slipping from you. Negativity is never really a part of you, rather it is an external reality that can be shed and discarded. You are not your mistakes or shortcomings! You are a pure and righteous soul. All Tumah, sins and 'failures' of your past year are dissolving in the living waters of the holy Mikvah. Feel and appreciate the unburdened lightness of your being.

Step Three: As your head emerges from the water in your final immersion, not only is the past washed away, but it is also transformed. You are a new you, filled with resolve and empowerment to live a higher and deeper life in the coming year. You are now ready to enter Yom Kippur like a pure, brilliantly shining angel, refreshed and renewed.

Every Day

Every night as we go to sleep we are entering a semi-state of death. Tumah is the world of darkness, deadness, lack of movement and separation. Therefore, after rising in the morning, many have the custom to immerse in the Mikvah to help them properly and smoothly transition from night, sleep and 'death', into light, alertness and vitality.

Step One: Perhaps you're still feeling tired or sleepy. Non-judgmentally recognize the sensations in your body. Notice that today is a brand new day with new possibilities, and that what happened yesterday or in the past is no absolute indication of how your day will unfold today. Look at your life and your situation up until today.

Step Two: Immerse fully in the restorative, regenerative waters and feel the infinite potential that the waters of the Mikvah are offering you. You are hovering within the primordial Womb of Creation, at one with the Divine desire to create infinite possibilities and to 'become'. Now, in this moment, under the water, you too have the power of *Ein Sof* / Infinity to become so much more of who you essentially already are.

Step Three: As your head is moving out of the water in your final immersion, have the Kavanah that you are in this moment reaching an even higher level of *Teharah* / purity and light, you are open and connected to the Source of all Life. You are awake, excited, enlivened and empowered to engage life fully and meet the new day with hope, faith, positivity and freshness. No matter what happened the day or days before, today is a new day, a new beginning, a new start.

〜〜〜

Erev Shabbos

Shabbos is a glimmer of the World to Come. On Shabbos, we enter the gentle, unitive world of 'water' and leave behind the aggressive, clamoring world of 'fire'.

Throughout the work-week we are busy with the needs of our body, and perhaps even obsessively striving to make a living or to accumulate more and more wealth. The paradigm of the body is separation, and we may therefore feel, think, speak and act as if we are separate from Hashem and Hashem's Creation. To properly enter into Shabbos, the world of soul, we need to let go of our work-week manner of thinking, speaking and doing. To achieve this, many have the custom to immerse in the uplifting waters of the Mikvah. This practice mirrors the fact and prepares us for the reality that on Shabbos we are like fish in water, at one with the world around us and with HaKadosh Baruch Hu, submerged and swimming in a Divine space.

Step One: Begin by contemplating the events of the past week, review all of your thoughts, words and actions. Acknowledge and own them. Resolve to let go of your weekday consciousness, including any worries, doubts, anxieties or competitiveness.

Step Two: As you sink beneath the waters, feel all tension, lack and aggression slip away. The four walls of the Mikvah embracing you embodies the Four Letter Name of Hashem; your entire past week, the entire *Pekel* / package that is weighing you down is now being 'returned' to Hashem. You are totally free of work-week thoughts, actions and deeds. Now, immerse at least one more time, and feel the sweet Kedushah of Shabbos enveloping and suffusing your entire being.

Step Three: As your head is leaving the water, have Kavanah that Shabbos is bringing you a *Panim Chadashos* / new countenance; a holy new you, a fresh way of being, thinking, speaking and doing. As you exit the waters of the Mikvah in space, you are now prepared to enter the 'Mikvah of Time', the holy and restful day of Shabbos.

AFTERWORD

OUR SAGES TELL US THAT WE CAN SELL A SEFER TORAH / TORAH SCROLL — THE MOST VENERATED OBJECT, called "the delight of our eyes" (*Sanhedrin*, 102b) — to help raise funds for a marriage (*Megilah*, 27a). We can extend this principle to the endeavor of building a women's Mikvah, which as we have learned is necessary for marital intimacy; meaning that, if there is no other way to raise the funds, we can even sell a Sefer Torah and with that money, build a Mikvah so that married women can immerse monthly (*Igros Moshe*, Ohrach Chayim 1, 51:4). Certainly, building a Mikvah is a communal priority above building a *Shul* / Synagogue or purchasing a Sefer Torah, among other meritorious deeds (Chafetz Chayim, *Beis Yisrael* 3:8).

This illustrates just how essential the Mitzvah of Mikvah is for the flourishing of Jewish life. A women's Mikvah allows spouses to be intimate and bring new life to themselves, their families, their communities and the world.

Tumah, as explored in great length throughout this text, is a deadening spiritual effect within every transgression and every form of negativity. However, by immersing in a Mikvah, whether daily, weekly or upon certain special occasions, Tumah is eliminated, and we are elevated and exalted in the essential purity of being alive. Such is the phenomenal power of a small ritual pool.

Having explored the multi-dimensional potentials of the Mikvah in today's day and age, it is our hope and prayer that very speedily, we will merit a time when Hashem will "sprinkle purifying water upon you, and you shall be purified" (*Yechezkel*, 36:25). As the great sage, Rabbi Akiva said, "How fortunate are you, Yisrael / Israel: before whom are you purified, and who purifies you? It is your Father in Heaven, as it is stated, 'And *I* will sprinkle purifying water upon you, and you shall be purified.' [And who is the *I* referred to in this verse?] As it says, 'The Mikvah of Yisrael is Hashem' (*Yirmiyahu*, 17:13). Just as a Mikvah purifies the impure, so too, the Holy One, Blessed be He, purifies Yisrael" (*Yuma*, 85b).

May we merit to observe the fulfillment of this prophecy speedily, in our days, with the coming of Moshiach — *Kein Yehi Ratzon* / may it be Hashem's will.

OTHER BOOKS BY
RAV DOVBER PINSON

RECLAIMING THE SELF
The Way of Teshuvah

~~~

THE MYSTERY OF KADDISH
Understanding the Mourner's Kaddish

~~~

UPSHERNISH: THE FIRST HAIRCUT
*Exploring the Laws, Customs & Meanings
of a Boy's First Haircut*

~~~

A BOND FOR ETERNITY
Understanding the Bris Milah

~~~

REINCARNATION AND JUDAISM
The Journey of the Soul

~~~

INNER RHYTHMS
The Kabbalah of MUSIC

~~~

MEDITATION AND JUDAISM
Exploring the Jewish Meditative Paths

~~~

TOWARD THE INFINITE

THIRTY-TWO GATES
into the Heart of Kabbalah & Chassidus

~~~

THE PURIM READER
The Holiday of Purim Explored

~~~

EIGHT LIGHTS
8 Meditations for Chanukah

~~~

THE IYYUN HAGADAH
An Introduction to the Haggadah

~~~

PASSPORT TO KABBALAH
A Journey of Inner Transformation

~~~

THE FOUR SPECIES
The Symbolism of the Lulav & Esrog

~~~

THE BOOK OF LIFE AFTER LIFE
(This book is an updated and expanded version of the book; Jewish Wisdom of the Afterlife)

THE GARDEN OF PARADOX:
The Essence of Non – Dual Kabbalah

~~~~

The Meditation Series:
BREATHING & QUIETING THE MIND

VISUALIZATION AND IMAGERY:
Harnessing the Power of our Mind's Eye

SOUND AND VIBRATION
Tuning Into the Echoes of Creation

~~~~

THE POWER OF CHOICE:
A Practical Guide to Conscious Living

~~~~

MYSTIC TALES FROM THE EMEK HAMELECH

~~~~

INNER WORLDS OF JEWISH PRAYER

~~~~

WRAPPED IN MAJESTY
Tefillin – Exploring the Mystery

The Spiral of Time Series:

~~~~

THE SPIRAL OF TIME:
Unraveling the Yearly Cycle & Rosh Chodesh

THE MONTH OF SHEVAT:
Elevating Eating & The Holiday of Tu b'Shevat

THE MONTH OF IYYAR:
Evolving the Self & The Holiday of Lag B'Omer

THE MONTHS OF TAMUZ/AV:
Embracing Brokenness, Transforming Darkness

The Three Weeks: From the 17th of Tamuz until the 9th of Av & Tu b'Av

THE MONTH OF TEVES:
Refining Relationships: Elevating the Body